The Minsk Ghetto

THE MINSK GHETTO

Soviet-Jewish Partisans
Against the Nazis

Hersh Smolar

HOLOCAUST LIBRARY
New York

Translated from the Yiddish by Max Rosenfeld

Library of Congress Cataloging-in-Publication Data

Smolar, Hersh, 1905-
The Minsk Ghetto.

Translation of: Fun Minsker geto.
"Holocaust Library."
1. Jews — Byelorussian S.S.R. — Minsk — Persecutions. 2. Holocaust, Jewish
(1939-1945) — Byelorussian S.S.R. — Minsk — Personal narratives. 3. World War,
1939-1945 — Underground movements, Jewish — Byelorussian S.S.R. — Minsk.
4. Smolar, Hersh, 1905-   . 5. Minsk (Byelorussian S.S.R.) — Ethnic relations.
I. Title.
DS135.R93M5913   1989   947'.652   LC# 87-81216
ISBN: 0-89604-068-2 (Cloth)
ISBN: 0-89604-069-0 (Paper)

Cover design by The Appelbaum Company

Printed in the United States of America

Published by
Holocaust Library
216 West 18th Street
New York, NY 10011

HOLOCAUST PUBLICATIONS

A non-profit organization

Publishers of the

HOLOCAUST LIBRARY

STATEMENT OF PURPOSE

The Holocaust spread across the face of Europe just a few decades ago. The brutality then unleashed is still nearly beyond comprehension. Millions of innocents — men, women and children — were consumed by its flames.

The goal of Holocaust Publications, a non-profit organization founded by survivors, is to publish and disseminate works on the Holocaust. These will include survivors' accounts, testimonies and memoirs, historical and regional analyses, anthologies, archival and source documents and other relevant materials that will help shed light on this cataclysmic era.

These books and studies will be made available to the general public, scholars, researchers, historians, teachers and students. They will be used in Holocaust Resource Centers, libraries and schools, synagogues and churches. They will help foster an increased awareness of the Holocaust and its implications. They will help to preserve the memory for posterity and to enable this awesome time to be better understood and comprehended.

Holocaust Library
216 West 18th Street
New York, NY 10011
212-463-7988

TABLE OF CONTENTS

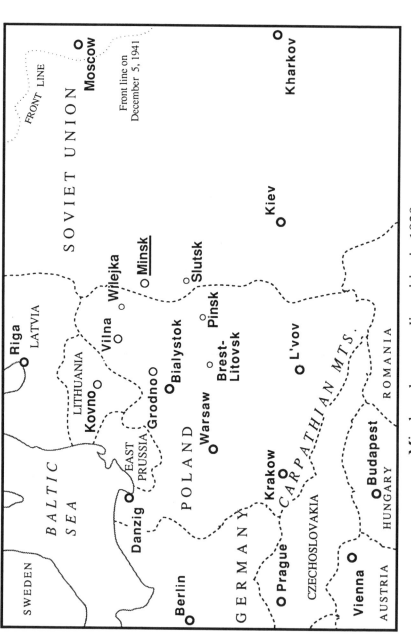

Minsk and surrounding cities in 1939

For the Second Time

After almost forty years I find myself writing again about the largest ghetto of "indigenous" Soviet Jews in Minsk, capital of the Byelorussian Republic, which was occupied by the Hitlerites in World War II. (I use the word "indigenous" Soviet Jews to distinguish them from the Jews who, at the outbreak of the war, had been living under Soviet rule for barely two years — in Bialystok, Vilna, Lwow, Riga, Kovno and a number of other cities.)

The first time I wrote about the struggle, agony and destruction of the Minsk ghetto was at the end of 1944, only a few months after I returned from the Partisan forests. What moved me to do so was, first of all, the urge to transmit to both the surviving Jews and the general Soviet public the truth about what happened in the only Jewish ghetto in the Soviet Union, a ghetto which resisted the Nazis until the moment when, after the uprising in the Warsaw ghetto, the German high command ordered all the ghettos in Eastern Europe destroyed, without exception. That was in the summer and autumn of 1943.

What also motivated me was the general reluctance of leaders of the Communist Party and the Soviet government of Byelorussia to acknowledge anything that had to do with the Jews under German occupation, plus the unconcealed hatred of those who spread the anti-Semitic libel that the Jews had evaded military service in the war, that they had been hiding in the hinterlands (Tashkent was supposed to symbolize that), that Jews had simply gone out and bought the awards and medals they had supposedly earned in action on the war fronts.

My book on the Minsk ghetto, published by Emes in Moscow (10,000 copies in Yiddish; 50,000 in Russian) was intended to refute that libel and to demonstrate the particularly tragic fate of the Soviet Jews caught in that ghetto and the role of the Minsk Jews in creating the first ghetto combat organization in occupied Europe, as well as the general resistance center for the city of Minsk. In doing this, I relied on my own memory (I had been kept informed of everything that happened in the ghetto), and on the memory of

[1]

many fellow combatants who had been active in the Minsk ghetto undergrund and with the partisans. (As secretary of the combat organization in the Minsk ghetto I received daily reports both from couriers and from the secretaries of the various groups in the ghetto, as well as from the Judenrat, the ghetto police and the Labor Office.) Every name, date and event in my manuscript was checked with all these people. My book thus became a collective testimony of documentary significance.

The conditions prevailing at that time, however, did not permit me to tell the whole truth, either about the anti-Semitism displayed by the general resistance movement toward the ghetto combat organization, or about the anti-Semitism in the partisan ranks, or about the specific problems encountered by the indigenous Soviet Jews when they found themselves behind ghetto walls, problems which in great measure stemmed from the Soviet past and affected the Jews during the German occupation as well.

It happened that in 1948, when the Jewish Anti-Fascist Committee was liquidated, along with all the Jewish institutions that still existed, and when the Soviet Jewish writers, artists and cultural leaders were arrested, my book on the Minsk ghetto was also "liquidated." As a result, copies of the book became a rarity. (One such "rescued" copy was brought to me as a gift by General David Dragunski, twice decorated Hero of the Soviet Union, when he came to Poland for the 15th anniversary of the Warsaw Ghetto uprising.)

As I now set about, for the second time, to retrieve from my memory the events of that terrible period in the history of our people, I am thinking first of all of the younger generation of Soviet Jews, who know very little about the suffering of their parents in the ghetto and even less about the history of their armed resistance against the Germans.

The Minsk ghetto, unlike the ghettos of Warsaw, Bialystok, Lodz, Vilna and other cities, has not had the good fortune of attracting the interest of researchers and historians. Yet the intervening time and the accumulated archival material would serve to elucidate both the common and the specific features in the history of one of the largest ghettos in occupied Europe. (A scholarly work, *Ghetto of Minsk, Struggle and Annihilation* (in Hebrew) was written by Haim Harpaz, graduate student at Tel Aviv University, who made use of German documents from the Yad Vashem archives. This work is still unpublished.)

Those works that have been published so far in various countries about the resistance and destruction of the Jews in the ghettos of Eastern Europe rely heavily on the data about Minsk in my previously mentioned book, as well as in the personal testimony of Anna Matshis, L. Gleiser, F. Shapiro and Gretshanik, all of which was included in *The Black Book* edited by Vasily

Grossman. These data are copiously cited in Moshe Kaganovich's two-volume *The Wars of the Jewish Partisans in Eastern Europe*. Fragments on the Minsk ghetto can be found in J. Grinshtein's *Light from Jubilee Square* (Hebrew) and in A. Sluchowski's *From the Ghetto to the Forest*, in the Hebrew anthology *Sefer HaPartizanim HaYehudim*. Separate chapters are devoted to the Minsk ghetto in the books by Yuri Suhl and Reuben Ainsztein (both in English) and by the historian Lucien Steinberg (in French). The historians Isaiah Trunk and Sholom Cholawski have written about the Judenrat in Minsk. Soviet historians, especially from Byelorussia, generally note the existence of the combat organization in the Minsk ghetto, but they do it in a truncated, fragmentary way, although the ghetto organization is featured prominently in the minutes of meetings of the combat center for the entire city of Minsk.

Soviet works of belles-lettres on the theme of the Minsk ghetto have appeared in Russian, Byelorussian and Yiddish. *The Bloody Banks of the Niemiga*, by Vladimir Karpov, reflects the events of the ghetto. Fragments about the ghetto combat organization and its influence on the general struggle in Minsk can be found in the work (in Russian and Byelorussian) by Ivan Novikov called *Ruins Shoot Straight*. Yiddish books by Hirsh Dobin, Isaac Plotner, Hirsh Kamenetski, Moyshe Teif and Haim Maltinski are devoted to the Minsk ghetto.

With the growth of anti-Semitism in the Soviet Union, the martyrdom and resistance story of the Soviet Jews in World War II is more and more being falsified and suppressed. Propaganda depicting the Jews as "partners of the Nazis" grows more and more brazen. The younger generation of Jews, now striving to find its roots and its identity, has been deprived of access to the truth about their fathers, hundreds of thousands of whom took part in the worldwide war of retribution against the monstrous Hitlerites on all battlefronts, in the ghettos and in the ranks of the partisans.

In this second effort to write the history of the mass anti-Nazi battle of he Jews of Minsk, and of the destruction of the largest ghetto of Soviet Jews, the author had foremost in mind the surviving Jews and their children, who were promised, as a testament from one generation to the next, that never would the martyrdom of their murdered families be forgotten. The other part of that testament was that they must learn from the fighting history of their parents, brothers and sisters, everywhere and always to expose and to confront the modern heirs of Nazism and anyone else who ever again threatens the life of the Jewish people.

Road Without an Exit

The road from Bialystok to Minsk is a bit more than 400 kilometers — if you were measuring the normal road. But there no longer was a normal road for those people who were fleeing eastward in panic, on foot, to look for a place to hide from the onrushing enemy. The highway was jammed with demolished trucks, smashed cannon, discarded machine-guns. Now and again, aircraft with the Nazi emblem swooped over this pile of assorted weapons. They flew so low that we could see the mocking, contemptuous faces of the flying German thugs. They made one foray after another, "playfully" firing their machine-guns into groups of terror-stricken people on the road, mostly women holding children by the hand or in their arms.

Usually the people walked — or strayed — on village byways. For a short distance only, they might catch a ride with a group of Soviet officers who expected to learn — from me, the local man — how to get to a certain point in the city. Although they all carried military maps, they would run their fingers nervously over the map, put it back into their new leather cases and mutter, "Devil only knows where the place is!" The maps had been prepared by the Soviet general staff, but they were useless in the area these officers now found themselves in, which was *on the way back* to the east. The maps, with all the customary and requisite military markings, showed only the way toward East Prussia, in accordance with Stalin's assurance that the war would be waged only on enemy soil. . .

On this "march" I kept meeting acquaintances who, like me, had missed the last train out of the Bialystok station. We had never expected that on the second day of the war, the 23rd of June, 1941, we would have to flee — on foot — to put some distance between ourselves and the enemy, who was racing ahead at an incredible pace. We were not ready for that. I couldn't help but recall a meeting in Bialystok a year earlier, at Count Branitzki's palace, where the regional offices of the Communist Party and the Soviets were housed. The leaders of the region had gathered there, along with the activists in all the Soviet organizations and institutions, to hear a report on the international situation. The speaker was P. K. Ponomarenko, the most important man in the Byelorussian Soviet Republic, the Boss himself, the Premier and First Secretary of the Communist Party of Byelorussia. His words were remarkably self-assured, as if his hands held the key to all the problems that had arisen in a world undermined by Hitlerism, problems that were especially disturbing to the people in this city so close to the part of Poland occupied by the Nazis.

As usual, to the accompaniment of loud, prolonged applause, the speaker was about to step off the platform, when suddenly a woman's voice rose above the din. She wanted to ask a question, she said. Everyone looked around to see where this extraordinary display of courage was coming from — imagine! — asking the Chief Executive of the Republic a question after he had ended a report in which he had already solved all the problems so clearly and decisively! This woman with the haggard face and bobbed grey hair was so small that it was hard to see her in the crowd. But she managed to push her way through, and without even waiting for permission from the chairman, she began to ask her question in a mixture of Russian and Polish.

The audience stared at her curiously, not knowing who she was. But we, a small group of activists from the Communist underground in Poland, knew her. We had merited an invitation to this meeting because we had once belonged to the Soviet Communist Party. We certainly knew who this woman was, this "naive" woman who was'nt even aware that at such a meeting one does not ask questions of a high Soviet leader. Her name was Maria Eiger, of the family of Akiva Eiger. When she was arrested in pre-war Poland for Communist activity, the Polish press had dubbed her "The Jewish Princess." Her parents were wealthy Jews from Lodz, but she herself led a near-ascetic life devoted to underground political work. We knew that her mother made it a practice to come periodically to "Serbia," the women's prison in Warsaw, with a wagonload of food for all the prisoners. That was Maria's wish.

At this meeting, Maria did more than ask a question, however. She had something to tell. She was one of the last people to escape from Nazi-occupied Warsaw to the Soviet city of Bialystok. German officers in Warsaw, she said, had been boasting openly, "Soon we'll be there too" — meaning the Soviet zone. People in the West had heard about concentrations of German army units that had been moved from occupied Europe to the Soviet borders. Finally Maria Eiger asked her question:

"Does the leadership of the Soviet Union know about this and what do they think about it?"

[5]

With obvious annoyance, Ponomarenko answered her brusquely in the following words:

"We need only twenty-four hours to get the whole Soviet people up on its feet."

Not for twenty-four hours, but for three days and three nights the feet of countless armed and unarmed men and women had done nothing but run as fast as they could to stay ahead of the Germans, who still managed to get in front of them with their troops and their aircraft.

At Volkovisk our feet refused to obey us any longer. Across the buckled railroad tracks lay a string of wrecked cars. Our suspicion that the victims indside those cars might be our own people whom we had managed to send out on the then still functioning train forced our aching feet to keep on moving.

It was Igaiev, First Secretary of the Bialystok Regional Committee of the Party, who had promised us that all the writers and their families would be evacuated immediately. Special trains were assigned for some fifty Yiddish writers and a smaller number of Byelorussian and Polish writers. To Igaiev's question: "Are you going with them?" I replied that I had been mobilized into the army and therefore had to stay where I was. (I was then secretary of the Writers Union.)

Between Igaiev and me a unique relationship had developed that could not be made public. The "westerners" were regarded by the emissaries from the east as "unreliables" who should be treated with suspicion and kept at arm's length. Igaiev, however, made it possible for me to kep in touch with him directly by telephone, so that I wouldn't have to go through the secretaries. This close bond between us — though physically we kept our distance — was due to something that had happened earlier.

In one of our conversations Igaiev discovered that I knew a good friend of his youth from Minsk, a Jew who was assigned in the 1930s to illegal political work in western Byelorussia. This friend had then been sentenced to a term in a Soviet labor camp on some absurd charge. "Let's get him out of there," Igaiev said to me one day — words quite uncharacteristic of any Soviet citizen, let alone one with the rank of First Secretary of the Party Regional Committee. Igaiev asked me to write a character reference that would prove his friend's ideological stability, his loyalty and steadfastness under the most difficult conditions of Polish police terror. Together, Igaiev and I celebrated the news that my letter had helped to get him released. During the general disruption on that first day of the war, Igaiev showed his concern for us when he ordered special trains for all the writers and their families.

[6]

He advised me, also, to keep in constant touch with him, so that I would have up-to-the-minute knowledge of the changing situation. But to several telephone queries during the course of that day his only response was: "We are all at our posts."

Together, David Richter (a seasoned trade union leader) and I translated Molotov's speech into Yiddish and when it was printed both of us went up and down the now deserted Bialystok streets and pasted the sheets on the walls. The message contained Molotov's comforting promise: "One day there will again be joy on our streets."

Long before that happened, however, hope of a quick victory had begun to fade, a hope that had arisen during the first months after the Soviet army entered the western regions. The hope for a normal Jewish life — Soviet style, of course — seemed at first to have a basis in reality. Refugees began bringing over their families, sending food packages to the "other side." There were many Jews friendly to the Soviet Union who registered to come and work in remote Soviet industrial areas. Bialystok became a leading cultural center, with Yiddish state schools, a Yiddish state theater, a Yiddish newspaper.

It wasn't long, however, before things began looking totally different. Soviet reality took over, bringing with it keen disappointment and much suffering. Masses of Jews who had come from Poland were now sent to the east on the pretext that "Bialystok, a border city, is not safe, especially for Jews with 'special paragraphs' in their passports, or who did not even wish to accept Soviet passports; they have all become suspect." Arrests took place on the basis of denunciations. We were shocked by the arrest of Aaron Berezinski, Yiddish novelist and an editorial associate of the *Byalystoker Shtern*. Even Igaiev threw up his hands and advised us not to intervene.

Particularly depressing was the meeting in Abram Bukowitsh's room with Yitzhok Nusinov, who was our professor of literature at Moscow Western University. Peretz Markish, who was also there, was furious, but all they could tell us was what they had learned in Minsk from Pantieleimon Ponomarenko himself: Jewish life in Bialystok and in the other western regions would be no different than it was anywhere else in the Soviet Union.

And that's precisely what happened. A process of Russification began in the Yiddish schools. The Yiddish daily newspaper became a sheet with obligatory bulletins translated from the Russian. The Yiddish theater began to wane. And all this was accompanied by late-night searches and seizures. It even happened to veteran Jewish textile workers, who were charged with being Bundists or Trotzkyites. A mood of hopelessness enveloped the old revolutionary trade union leaders who had previously challenged foreign press reports about the decimation of Jewish life. "Malicious propaganda by enemies of the Soviet Union," they had called it.

When the news reached us from Minsk, shortly before Hitler's invasion of the Soviet Union, that the poet Zelig Axelrod, a good friend of mine, the prose writer Eli Kagan, and the literary critic Grisha Beryozkin had all been arrested, an abyss of despair overwhelmed us. Axelrod, a close friend of the murdered poet Izzy Charik, knew very well what had happened in 1937 to the Yiddish writers of Byelorussia. Nevertheless, he had helped us in every way he could, as though he were oblivious to the risk he was taking. He paid for that generosity with his life. A bullet from the gun of a guard killed him one night while the prisoners in the Minsk jail were being moved. Kagan and Beryozkin managed to escape.

Hitler's attack suddenly muted all these woes, cruelly underlining the hideous trap we were in, encircled as we were by the Germans, with absolutely no way out.

What was to be done?

It was after midnight when I telephoned Igaiev. His reply was the usual one, although his voice was agitated: "We are all at our posts. . . Do whatever you think best."

By three o'clock that morning, Igaiev's telephone no longer answered. The main street of the city was jammed with speeding trucks overloaded with furniture and household goods — Soviet "apparatchiks" getting out as fast as they could. Not one of them offered to pick me up.

At the deserted station a Polish railroad worker told me, with feigned sympathy, that unfortunately I had just missed the last train. . .

On the long march we soon learned that the German army had already caught up with us. Squads of young soldiers in trucks rode by us like tourists on holiday, their shirtsleeves rolled up and their collars open to the sun, which was draining the last bit of strength from the homeless, hopeless refugees. From one tank that had slowed down — the officer had taken a fancy to my boots — I heard perfect Russian being spoken. Several times the German loudspeaker repeated that this was the voice of Stalin's son, who had been taken prisoner. The leitmotif of all this mystification was:

"All is lost! Surrender!"

What was to be done?

David Richter, his son Heniek and I, marching on bare, bloody feet, made it to Slonim. Obeying German orders, Jews there were rushing toward the Great Synagogue. "All Jewish males must report to the Great Synagogue between 6 p.m. and 6 a.m." The congestion inside was indescribable.

What was to be done?

[8]

Richter made his decision: "There's no use going any further. Wherever we go, the enemy is there ahead of us."

I decided nonetheless to keep moving, to try to reach Minsk, perhaps make contact with someone there who could help me get to the front, help me find some way out of this trap.

On the road to Baranowitsh the Germans were rounding up men. At the Jewish cemetery they had erected a camp for war prisoners (we recognized them by their shaved heads) and for Jews (whoever had the word *Yevrei* on his internal Soviet passport.) Mieczslaw Kozak and I (he was a Polish union leader) tried to escape from the camp by crawling under the fence. The guards heard us and started firing, but missed. We made it safely to the other side.

Among the crowds on the roads we met many people whom we knew — they had made the same calculations we did — in the big city perhaps we could find a way out. But we also met people who were coming back — there was no place left to run to. Kozak and I were joined by Marila Dziekan, a trade union leader from the coal regions. She and Kozak were my "cover" — traveling with them I was not a Jew.

But in a village where we stopped for the night, a German officer yelled at my companions:

"Why don't you get rid of that kike! He and his kind are to blame for this war!" I remember thinking how good his Polish was.

I ran, zigzagging, bracing myself for the bullet. But he didn't fire.

The next morning, on the road to Minsk, I met my companions again. Kozak had saved a chunk of bread for me. Marila avoided my eyes. I wanted very much not to be a burden to them. I made my decision. But I would not be able to carry it out until I came to Minsk.

In Minsk — For the Third Time

For many years I had been connected with this "Jewish" city. At first, only from a distance. From Kiev and Kharkov, threads of friendship ran to the young writers group in Minsk, to the youth newspaper edited in a popular style by Yankl Rubinchik, to the entire Yiddish milieu there, which was so different from that in Kiev, Kharkov and other cities in the Ukraine because of its manifest *Soviet* Yiddishkayt (Jewishness). At conferences and consultations in Moscow I had occasion to meet often with the "Minskers."

In 1928, the first time I was ever in Minsk, I was forbidden to go out and look at the city or to meet with any of my acquaintances. For days at a time I sat in my hotel room reading Polish underground materials and waiting for a moonless night so I could steal across the border to Poland.

The second time I met Minsk was six years later, and again I was warned: "Don't move around the city too much. Avoid meeting friends." I had come from Poland in accordance with a decision that I spend some time in a safe place, because the Polish police were hot on my trail.

Now, on my third "visit" to Minsk I told my two Polish companions all about this and asked that we stop for a moment at a gutted building on Moscow Street near the little railroad bridge.

Six years earlier we had all moved into that house with assumed names, since we were leaders in the Communist underground in Vilna and Bialystok, Pinsk and Grodno, Brisk and Slonim. For six years we enjoyed complete safety, not even thinking about the possibility of falling into the hands of the Polish political police, until the decision was made that we could return to Poland. We were involved in the kind of work (in Minsk itself and outside the city) that demanded total secrecy — delivering lectures, arranging seminars, running the school to train cadres for the underground, writing leaflets and pamphlets, editing periodicals in five languages (Byelorussian, Yiddish, Polish, Russian, Lithuanian), training people to work in the two underground printing-houses in Vilna and Bialystok (the Polish political police never did uncover them).

Now only the skeleton of that building remained. There were no steps, so

I couldn't go up to what had been my room. There were no traces of a past that had been eradicated, even before the war, by the Stalinist decree condemning the people of the underground as provocateurs and Polish espionage agents.

On Sovietska Street the tallest building in Minsk — "Government House" — stood absolutely intact. But on the ground in front of the building, the Lenin monument lay prostrate. All the other buildings were only shells. We had been hoping that the Writers House had also been spared, but I could barely recognize the place. Only the front wall was still standing, and here the three of us stopped to read the words which opened a little crack in the cordon of my own desperation.

This is what we were reading, in German or Byelorussian:

ORDER*
Concerning the Establishment of a Jewish Quarter in the City of Minsk:
1.
Effective today, the date of this order, a separate section of the city will be set aside where only Jews shall reside.
2.
Within three days of the posting of this Order, all Jewish inhabitants of the City of Minsk must move into the Jewish Quarter. After that time, any Jew found in the non-Jewish area of the city will be arrested and severely punished. Non-Jewish inhabitants who now live inside the borders of the Jewish Quarter must immediately leave. If there are no dwellings in the non-Jewish area that have been vacated by Jews, the Housing Office of the Minsk municipal government will provide other dwellings.
3.
It is permissible to move household goods. Anyone caught taking goods belonging to someone else, or stealing, will be shot.
4.
The Jewish Quarter is bordered by the following streets: Kolvirt Alley to Kolvirt Street, along the creek to Niemiga Street, excluding the Pravoslavna Church, to Republikaner Street and the side-streets Shorna, Kolektorna, Mebl-Alley, Perekop, Kizova, the Jewish cemetery, Obutkova, Second Apanska-Alley, Zaslavski, to Kolvirt.
5.
The Jewish Quarter, after the Jews move into it, must be separated from the rest of the city by a brick wall, to be built by the inhabitants of the Jewish Quarter. For this purpose, building materials must consist of bricks from uninhabited or destroyed buildings.
6.
Jews from the Jewish labor brigades are forbidden to be in the non-Jewish

*This is translated from the Byelorussian text. Although in Byelorussian, Jews are designated as *Yavrei*, in this Order (as in all Byelorussian publications of the Nazi collaborators) the anti-Semitic appellation *zhidi* or *zhid* was used. (H.S.)

areas. These brigades may leave their quarter, with special permission, to go to designated work places assigned by the Minsk municipal government. Violators of this order will be shot.

7.

Jews are permitted to enter and leave the Jewish Quarter through two streets only — Apansik and Ostrovski. Climbing over the wall is forbidden. The German sentries and the Police guards are under orders to fire at anyone who violates this order.

8.

Only Jews and members of German military units are permitted to enter the Jewish Quarter. Also, those who belong to the Minsk municipal government, but only on official business.

9.

The Judenrat is responsible for raising a fund of 30,000 *chervontsi* (form of currency equivalent to approximately $30,000) for expenses connected with the relocation from one quarter to the other. This sum, the interest rate on which will be set at a later date, must be brought to the Cashier of the municipal administration, #28 Karl Marx Street, within 12 hours after the issuance of this Order.

10.

The Judenrat must immediately give to the Housing Office of the municipal government a report of all dwellings in the non-Jewish areas that Jews vacate and that have not yet been occupied by Aryan (non-Jewish) tenants.

11.

Order in the Jewish Quarter will be maintained by special Jewish police units. (A separate Order concerning this will be issued shortly.)

12.

Complete responsibility for the final relocation of the Jews into their Quarter belongs to the Judenrat of the City of Minsk. Any evasion of this Order will be most severely punished.

(signed) Field Commandant

The word "ghetto" was not used even once in this Order, but when I asked a Jew dragging a load of bundles on a hand-cart, "Where are you going," he pointed to the Order pasted on a nearby wall and said, "To the ghetto."

It was the Jews who came from Poland — the "refugees" — who brought this concept with them. The Jews of Minsk soon adopted it and explained its origin this way:

"Ghetto? Probably comes from the word *get* (Yiddish, divorce). They are going to divorce us from everything around us, from our neighbors, from our fellow-workers."

On another wall hung a second Order from the Military Field Commandant, concerning the "yellow patch." With their well known German precision, this Order specified the size of the patch and on what part of the clothing it must be sewn. And then came the familiar coda: For disobeying this Order the punishment is death. . .

Now the three of us sit on the still intact little bridge at the old Writers House. What my Polish traveling-companions are thinking, I don't know. But when I ask Marila to cut a piece of cloth from my greenish-yellow sack, so I can use it for a patch, they accept it as a natural thing. It is no longer possible for them to "cover" me, and there is nowhere now for the three of us, traveling together, to go. They, the Aryans, will look for a corner for themselves, and maybe some kind of work to support themselves.

And beyond that? For them the Order doesn't apply — that Order which is pushing me toward the only road that remains open. . . into the ghetto.

Along with a group of Jews carrying their household goods on their backs, or on carts, I enter the "Jewish Quarter. . . "

First Steps in the Ghetto

After more than twenty years of Soviet rule there were no longer any "Jewish neighborhoods" in Minsk. Jews resided in all parts of the city, urban and suburban — in Lachowka and Komorowka, in Perespa, Kalwaria and Serebrianka. This was clearly evident in the long lines of people heading toward the ghetto area from many directions. They came with hand-carts, on wagons with and without horses (usually without) loaded down with household goods, converging on narrow Komsomolska Street. From there the road led to Niemiga and Ostrovski Streets (past the Russian Orthodox Church), to the designated border of the ghetto. The noise there was deafening; the congestion and the yelling were indescribable.

"Why is everybody in such a hurry? Why all the pushing and shoving?"

A middle-aged, long-bearded man looked at me curiously and decided at once that I was not "from around here," because who didn't know that the last stage of relocation to the Jewish Quarter was in progress and that the oft-repeated formula, "punishment by death," was more than merely a warning. Jews had heard stories that on the day after the Germans occupied Minsk, they left behind a special group to murder and pillage, to put the fear of death into the population of this city in flames. The German army had advanced further east than Minsk, to Borisov and Orsha, and was on its way to Smolensk. Masses of Jews who had left the city on foot had returned only to fall into the hands of the murderers. Posters announced that "a hundred Jew-Bolsheviks had been shot." A new Order decreed that all men between the ages of 15 and 45 must register immediately. As usual, failure to do so was punishable by death.

On every street, soldiers with metal "half-moons" around their necks searched and seized men and boys with no discrimination as to national origin. As a rule, the Germans could not tell, from outward appearances, who was a Jew and who was not. As a result, there were men of diverse nationalities among those rounded up. These were sent to Drozdy, a camp outside the city. Prisoners with close-cropped hair were sent to the special war prisoners camp in Masiukovshtshina.

[14]

Out into the open field at Drozdy, under the blazing sun, the Hitlerites drove about 140,000 men and ordered them to sit on the ground. Anyone attempting to stand up was shot on the spot. Men died of thirst, but the slightest movement in the direction of the nearby stream drew the rat-tat-tat of a machine-gun or automatic rifle. Soon a specially selected group of prisoners appeared, mostly "ethnic Germans" from along the Volga, who dragged away the dead. This happened so frequently that the prisoners stopped reacting to the horror.

More and more often, women and children came to the camp, bringing food and clothing (even women's clothing, for their men to use in possible escape attempts), or civilian clothing for the captured soldiers. The Germans kept chasing them away, even firing their guns in the air, but the crowds of women around the camp grew larger every day.

Several days later came the Order to separate the Jews from the rest of the prisoners. At first, most of the Jewish prisoners did not realize what the intent of the Order was. Only a few sensed the danger and did not obey the decree. They stayed where they were, "covered" by Byelorussian or Russian friends. But even at that early stage there were scoundrels who "fingered" Jews to the Germans and were rewarded with an extra bowl of soup or a pack of tobacco. There were also mornings when informers were found on the ground strangled to death.

On the fifth day, all civilians except Jews were allowed to go free. War prisoners were sent to the camp at Masiukovshtshina, leaving only Jews at Drozdy. Then came the Order to separate Jews of the "educated professions" from the mass of other prisoners. People thought the Germans would probably put the Jewish engineers, technicians, architects, physicians and artists to work. About 3000 Jews reported themselves in this category, including some who claimed falsely that they were graduates of secondary schools.

The next Order was therefore very surprising: "All physicians and hospital workers step forward!" No one had anticipated what awaited the Jewish intellectuals. It never occurred to anyone that the first objective of the Nazis was to get rid of people who might lead a resistance movement. The Jews did not understand why the small group of Jewish doctors was sent back into the mass of Jewish prisoners. (Most of the doctors had been mobilized into the Soviet army in the very first days of the Hitler invasion.) From their experience in Warsaw and other ghettos in Poland, the Germans knew that epidemics might break out as a result of the crowded conditions and the starvation in the Jewish Quarters. They were deathly afraid of the possible spread of these epidemics outside the ghetto. For a time, therefore, they spared the Jewish doctors.

[15]

Not until they were on the road out of Drozdy did the captured Jewish intellectuals realize that they were being taken not to Minsk but in the opposite direction. Months later we heard the terrifying word Trostynietz, the death camp where the prisoners were killed immediately or had been suffocated to death in the *dushegubky* (gassing vans) even before they got to the camp. At Trostynietz the bodies were piled up and burned. The Jewish intellectuals of Minsk were thus among the first victims of the Nazi mass murder machine. The rumor among the Jews of Minsk was that these men had been taken from Drozdy to various labor camps and that they would soon send word of their whereabouts. . .

After another few days all the Jews in Drozdy were moved to the Minsk prison, where they were "registered." The authorities seemed to be especially interested in the occupations of the Jews. From the prison all the Jews were taken to the nearby ghetto, where they began searching for their families. During the time the men were imprisoned, their wives and children were forced to leave their homes and find a place inside the ghetto. No new apartment buildings had been built in this area. On the streets and alleys to the right and left of "Jubilee Square," the only place in the area with a few trees, there were mostly one-story wooden cottages. (Even under Soviet rule they remained the private property of their owners.) Now there was an exchange with their non-Jewish owners, who had been given furnished Jewish homes in buildings that had not been destroyed. The Jews had to sell most of their furniture. In the crowded ghetto rooms there was really no space left.

Thousands of Jews, wearing patches of many shades of yellow, stood near the building on Masiukovshtshina Street outside the ghetto, where the Judenrat had temporary quarters. (Only older people recalled the prerevolutionary word "Kehillah.") Now it was not placards but Orders typed in Russian and signed by the Judenrat: "All Jews must register and receive a new Ghetto Passport." Without this document you could not get a place to live or food to eat, etc. Young women sat at tables outside the building and registered the Jews: family name, number of people in the family, occupation before the war, previous address, current address, and please show your Soviet internal passport. These registrations were not very strict. Any document would serve. This circumstance was utilized by many people, especially former Communist Party members, officials in the government apparatus, who used false documents that did not contain their correct names or previous positions.

I used just such a procedure to "legalize" myself — without any papers at all. On the road to Minsk, when I encountered the first German military units, I buried all my documents under a tree in a village where I had been locked up overnight by German gendarmes. Helping me in this process of legalizing myself were the first acquaintances I met in the Judenrat. Thereafter I was known in the ghetto as Yefim Stolyarevitsh.

The person who helped me was Joel Lifshitz. I had had a small part in the biography of this middle-aged man whom I barely recognized — so drastically had his appearance changed in the first few weeks of the occupation. With his long black beard he looked nothing at all like the young Jewish miner I had met in the Donetz Basin during the 1920s. Under my influence he had begun studying diligently. Years later I met him in Moscow as a student at Western University. After graduating from the university he worked in the Minsk daily Yiddish newspaper *Oktyober* and for a time was chairman of the Byelorussian Journalists Association.

"Why did you stay here?" I asked him. "You held such a high government position — why didn't you leave during the evacuation?"

His reply served as a key to my understanding of the situation. In the first days, the Judenrat registration revealed that there were more than 50,000 Jews in the ghetto. Only a week later the total had risen to 80,000. Three months later the facts showed that this number too had been underestimated. My next question was more general:

"For almost a whole week you had information about the onrushing German army. Why did so many Jews remain behind?"

At that point, from the lips of this veteran Communist and well known organizational leader came the accusation against the Communist Party and the Soviet government. His jet black eyes blazed angrily:

"They betrayed us. . . Like cowards, like deserters, they ran away from us. They didn't even warn us. . . They ordered us to dig trenches, anti-tank ditches. Disciplined, we carried out their orders. They themselves, however, ran away, their trucks loaded not with people but with their own possessions. . ."

Afterward I heard that terrible truth very often, even from non-Jews. On the walls of burned out buildings in the occupied city I later saw rhymed anti-Ponomarenko slogans, one of which ended with the words: PANTILEIMON — DUSHA Z TIEBA WOK! (Pantileimon — May Your Soul Depart from You!)

Decades later, Soviet historians attempted to "correct" that piece of history. In the words of the Minsk historian I. M. Ignatenko: "Plans were worked out to evacuate the population, industrial enterprises and government institutions. . . Thus, for example, on June 24th, more than ten caravans left for the Soviet hinterlands, consisting of people and material goods.

But it was not possible to carry out any mass evacuations." (Emphasis added. Cited in *Istoria KPSS*, #7, 1975, p. 59). We should again note here that the German army did not enter Minsk until the evening of June 28. No "industrial enterprises" were evacuated from Minsk — unless that refers to the "material goods" that belonged to the dignitaries themselves. . .

Joel Lifshitz took me into his "home" — a single room on Ostrovski Street — into which were crowded two families with small children. So I had a roof over my head, although more often than not, because of the terrible overcrowding, I spent the July-August nights in the courtyard, where the conversations with my neighbors, who helped me orient myself to the situation and to the mood among the Jews, usually lasted till daybreak.

Mornings I would walk through nearby gardens that had already been dug up by people foraging for vegetables. Here and there lay a half-rotten head of cabbage, a carrot, a radish — which helped me get through the day. Despite the risk, I crossed over with Joel's family to the "other side," where there was a bombed out molasses factory. Thousands of people drained the thick syrup from pipes and barrels. On another occasion I went with them to a bombed out warehouse where we found quantities of — castor oil. For a time we used this oil to fry potatoes as our "main meal."

Even before the ghetto was sealed off, a kind of barter trade began with peasants in the marketplace. Jews traded suits of clothing, dresses and household utensils for food. The bread-ration cards promised by the Judenrat were never issued. Instead, the Judenrat issued sacks of black flour to the hospital, the children's home and (first of all) to the Ghetto Police, which was called "militia" in accordance with Soviet nomenclature. Flour was also distributed to Jews who besieged the Judenrat building and protested to the "Kehillah people" at the top of their lungs.

In the Minsk ghetto there were practically no social distinctions among the Jews. The Soviet social order had leveled the entire population into "workers." The only distinction was the one that came with your particular job. This granted certain privileges to a section of government and Party employees in the form of food and clothing. There were almost no individuals who owned large amounts of capital. Soviet policy had extracted most of the gold and silver from the population — first by opening special stores where one could buy scarce products for those metals, and later by expropriating (through arrests and torture) inheritances that had been handed down from generation to generation. The latter method yielded silver and platinum forks and spoons, gold watches that had been given as wedding presents, gold rings and earrings, and in some cases, foreign currency left by relatives visiting from abroad or that had been sent over with someone else.

[18]

The main "valuta" in the barter-trade between ghetto and "the other side" was the *otrez* — a coupon that was exchangeable for cloth for men's suits or women's dresses. Many of the ghetto inhabitants owned these because, under Soviet conditions, an *otrez* was the safest "investment" for savings. During the period of the Minsk ghetto these coupons were in great demand.

I myself owned nothing at all. I had left Bialystok *"yak stoi"* as the Jews of Minsk say, with the shirt on my back. Hunger began to show in my face, in my gait. I would go to the Judenrat hoping to get a bowl of soup — rye flour in hot water — at the soup-kitchen for homeless people. Here I overheard all kinds of stories about the Judenrat, about its leaders and officials. Joel was of great help to me in sorting all this out. The truth is that the Minsk Judenrat, in the way it was established and the way it conducted itself, was *totally different* from the Judenrate in Poland and in the western regions that were taken over by the Soviets.

The Hitler policy as propounded by Alfred Rosenberg, *Reichs-Minister* for the occupied eastern territories, was supposed to use the Jews themselves for implementing many of the anti-Jewish decrees. But in Minsk, as a result of Soviet policy toward the Jews, this turned out to be an exceptional situation. In the Soviet Union there were no kehillahs such as existed in the Polish cities. There were thus no Jewish communal representatives who could have formed the basis for a Judenrat. Nor were there any Soviet Jewish institutions after the Stalinist purge in 1937, which hit the Yiddish cultural milieu in Minsk particularly hard. The German occupation authorities therefore had no alternative but to create a Judenrat with random persons.

Among the Jews themselves there were various explanations as to how the Military Commandant came to select Ilya Mushkin as the "Eldest of the Jews." Some said that Mushkin was among those who had been maltreated by the Soviet government in 1937 and that the Germans had more trust in such people. (Actually there were many in the civil administration "on the Russian side" who had been released from prisons and camps; these included criminal prisoners as well.) Another "theory" was that since Ilya Mushkin had occupied a high post in the Soviet trade apparatus (he was a Deputy Director in the Minsk Industrial Trade Organization), the Nazis believed he would be more highly regarded by the Jews and would be better able to carry out the German orders.

The truth was (as members of the Judenrat explained to me later) that the "election" took place in quite an accidental way. The Military Commandant stood on Karl Marx Street and a large group of Jews, rounded up for forced labor, were paraded past him. At one point the group was ordered to halt and line up in rows. The Commandant inspected the rows, staring intently into the frightened faces of the Jews, who saw only death in his eyes. But they heard no order to shoot. Instead, the Commandant wanted to know if any of them spoke German. No one responded. A second time, he demanded in a more menacing tone: 'Who can speak German?' The Jews looked at each other with fear and suspicion, wondering which one of them would volunteer. When the Nazi reached for his gun, Ilya Mushkin spoke up. He knew a little German, he said. . .

Mushkin returned from the Commandant's headquarters with a written Order appointing "the *Jude* Elias Mushkin" as "Elder of the Jews." The Order also stated that he must supply to the Commandant, in the shortest possible time, the names of individuals who would form the Jewish Council (Judenrat), which would be responsible for collecting a large sum of money, in Soviet rubles, to be paid as a "tax."

Ilya Mushkin consulted with his friends. They compiled a list of names of honest people who would act on behalf of the Jews in the ghetto. In accordance with Soviet practice, the Judenrat members divided up between them the management of the various departments. Mushkin took upon himself the handling of contacts with the German and local authorities. Hirsh Ruditzer, a former Soviet economist, dealt with labor matters and administered the Labor Exchange (as it was called, after an institution of the 1920s). It also fell to his lot to seal off he ghetto.

There was no brick wall built around the Minsk ghetto, as had been ordered by the Field Commandant. (The *Einsatzkommandos*, however, were quickly deployed around the ghetto, ready to wipe out the Jews of Minsk, as they had done at Kiev.) The Germans were not "oriented" toward a walled, well-ordered ghetto that would last a long time. The Minsk ghetto was instead, encircled by a fence of barbed wire. A main gate was set up at the end of Shorna Street, guarded by Germans of the SCHUPO *(Schutz Polizei)* and "militiamen" of the Jewish *Ordnungsdienst*. In time, smaller exits were designated for the labor columns. Here it was mostly the Jewish militia that stood guard. It was these latter exits that came to play a significant role in the life and resistance of the Minsk Jews.

Every day, German military officers came to Hirsh Ruditzer with new demands for various kinds of skilled workers. Very often, when Ruditzer could not provide the required number of specialists, they would beat him and threaten to shoot "the whole crowd" of Judenrat members. Unskilled workers — for mixing cement, for loading trucks, for cleaning buildings — these the Germans would round up on the street. Usually they were men and women who congregated outside the Judenrat office.

The internal labor section — those employed in the workshops inside the ghetto itself — was under the supervision of Judenrat member Goldin. In addition to the skilled workers, one could find in these shops individuals with a "political background," which meant that they had to try to steer clear of informers and avoid the Labor Exchange.

Dolski, the manager of the Housing Section, had a particularly difficult job. Dolski was well known in Minsk as a theater director. With a group of friends he conducted a survey of all the dwellings in the ghetto and tried to find shelter for everyone. "Never in my life did I expect to direct a show like this," he often complained.

The Relief Section, to which the Minsk Jews gave the Soviet-style title *Sobes* (an acronym for *Socialnoe Obespietshenie*, Social Insurance), was managed by a man named Zorow, a stage personality who had been awarded the title of "Meritorious Actor of the Republic." His possibilities of assisting people were exceedingly limited. It wasn't until a civil administration had been established in Minsk that he began to receive certain food products to help the poorest of the poor in the ghetto. Zorow had an assistant named Rosenberg, who managed the soup kitchen.

A very important role belonged to Ziama Serebrianski, who was in charge of the Jewish Police. Recruiting men that he knew personally, he set up two militia districts. The Jewish police wore no uniforms except a wide yellow armband (on the right arm). All members of the Judenrat were also required to wear this band.

With this kind of composition, the Judenrat soon began receiving some favorable recognition from the ghetto population, especially when it became known that Ilya Mushkin had managed to obtain from the German authorities a two-week extension — until August 1941 — in the deadline for moving into the ghetto. People started believing that it would be possible to nullify other decrees as well, that the Judenrat would be able to defend the interests of the ghetto Jews. So when the Judenrat appealed for contributions to the ghetto "tax" — collectors went door to door, describing the dangerous consequences of not turning the money over to the Germans by the specified date — people tried to give as much as possible. Hope arose that somehow life would be "normalized," even in the crowded conditions of the ghetto, even with all the burdensome decrees that were hurled at them every day, even with the brutal and degrading way people were treated in the labor columns.

During the nightly courtyard conversations, Jews who remembered the Germans from the First World War expressed the hope that things would change, that the present troubles were happening because there was no civil authority and the military officials were therefore acting on their own. As to the nature of the Third Reich, or what Hitler intended for the Jews in general and the Jews in the former Soviet territories in particular, about that the Jews of Minsk had no idea. They may have heard something from the *Zapadniki* — the Jews who had come from Poland and talked about Kristallnacht, when a thousand synagogues in Germany were burned to the ground, when 7500 Jewish businesses were vandalized and looted, when 20,000 German Jews were deported to concentration camps, but such rumors were regarded as highly improbable. After all, the Soviet press had never reported such things. Concepts such as Nazism and Fascism had disappeared from the Soviet press.

How could the Jews of Minsk have known that the first murderous act committed by the Germans on the morning after they occupied Minsk was the beginning of a daily, steady, continuous process of extirpation. During that first month the process did not yet bear a mass character. Individuals would vanish. Individuals were rounded up in the streets of the ghetto and taken to unknown destinations. Men were dragged out of their homes and supposedly taken to workplaces, but not one of them had ever returned. It happened with my friend Joel Lifshitz. For a long time his family waited in vain for news of him.

Most terrible of all were the night raids. Officially the Germans were not allowed into the ghetto at night without special permission. Several watch-towers were erected, from which local police guards would fire shots into the air to frighten away possible unwanted "visitors." This had no effect at all, however, on the groups of German soldiers — marauders — who more and more frequently began visiting the ghetto at night. They would break into houses, conduct "inspections," steal whatever came to hand. In some instances, they forced young Jewish women to dance naked before them. Such visits often ended in killings. The screams of the victims could be heard all over the ghetto. Jews began putting up barricades at the courtyard gates to keep out these night raiders. Fear and helplessness gripped the entire ghetto population.

What Is to Be Done?

I asked this question of myself, first of all, and for the second time in my life I could find no answer whatsoever. The first time that had happened was fourteen years earlier. I'd been spending a vacation in the Crimea and there was a disastrous earthquake. The ground split asunder, the sea pounded furiously, buildings simply crumbled. The balcony wall of my room collapsed. I barely managed to escape down the shaky stairs. People ran in panic from place to place, not knowing how to save themselves. The tremors kept recurring, now stronger, now weaker. Electric power was knocked out. Telephone communication was severed. No rescue ships stood outside the harbor. The situation seemed utterly hopeless.

During the first ghetto days our situation was similar. Nothing in my entire life-experience had prepared me to answer the question this time either: What was to be done? And the question in this instance, as in my previous experience, was not how to save myself alone. By that time I had already rejected two offers of a possible way out for myself. The suggestion came from a man named Senkewitsh, who was the former Director of the Party Center in Bialystok. Noticing me among a group of Jews that had been rounded up for forced labor, he waited until the attention of the German guard was distracted and whispered to me, "Rip off the yellow patch right now and follow me!" He had family in a nearby collective farm, he said, and would help me "wait there" until the Soviet army returned. I did not accept his offer.

I also declined the proposal of Lazar Fishman, whom I met at the Judenrat. In our home town he was the first Chairman of the temporary city administration after the Soviet army entered. He proposed that we "go back home" together. He had many good friends among the local Polish population there who would undoubtedly help us. Lazar Fishman never even managed to start on that road back. During one of the Nazi roundups he was caught in the net and we never saw him again.

I was overjoyed to meet the Yiddish writer Hirsh Dobin, an old friend of mine. He had found a place in the Jewish Children's Home, where he set up a shop to repair children's shoes; so far the Germans had let him alone. He offered to find a similar place for me, which would at least provide me with bread and soup. The most important thing I learned from him, however, was that Notke Wainhoyz was also "holed up" in the ghetto somewhere. Notke, whom I knew from the 1920s, was the former editor of the Yiddish children's newspaper published in Minsk. In Birobidjan he had managed the radio station and edited the Yiddish radio programs. With his vibrant temperament and his unfailing initiative he had helped tremendously in the cultural and communal work there.

In 1937 or 1938 he, Josef Rabin and Hirsh Dobin were arrested and sentenced for "the crime of Jewish nationalism." Immediately prior to the German invasion of the Soviet Union he managed to get back to Minsk, his home town. He had been my guest in Bialystok and whenever I came to Minsk I would stay with him. I enjoyed the long chats I had with his father, a building-trades worker, whose Yiddish was peppered with Minsk localisms.

Hirsh Dobin gave me Notke's address on New-Miasnitska Street. I hardly recognized him. His handsome, expressive face was now covered with dark, heavy wrinkles. All the fire had gone out of his eyes. Before I even said a word he went into the kitchen, brought out a loaf of bread and a bowl of lukewarm soup. At that point something happened that made the food stick in my craw. Notke's father, whom I remembered as a wise, cheerful man, suddenly shouted hysterically:

"What are you doing! We'll starve to death! You're giving away our last bit of food! We don't need any visitors!" And he looked at me with such mistrust that I instinctively began moving toward the door.

(Some time later, doctors told me that there were many such cases of hysteria in the ghetto. They stemmed from the fear of starvation and happened when the ghetto was first fenced in on all sides.)

Taking my arm, Notke eased me through a door leading up to the attic. This was his hiding-place. On an overturned box lay several sheets of writing paper covered with his handwriting. He also had a hidden radio up here on which he could pick up broadcasts from the Soviet front. I asked him what he was writing under these conditions. He handed me the manuscript. It was an angry account of his arrest and interrogation in Birobidjan. At that time I had not yet read anything about the "*Yezhovshchina*."* It left me with a feeling of depression that only deepened my feeling of hopelessness.

Notke Wainhoyz gave me the name of a "contact" who would help me find a way to keep body and soul together in the ghetto conditions. The

---

* The period during which N.I. Yezhov was head of the N.K.V.D. Soviet Secret Police.

"hunger-bloating" was becoming more and more evident. Marching home after a day's work with the forced labor battalions I frequently had to be supported by others. Notke's note was addressed to — the Chief of the ghetto police, Zyama Serebrianski. In their youth they had worked together in the Communist youth organization (Komsomol). Notke assured me that Serebrianski would do everything he possibly could for me and that I could trust him implicitly.

And, indeed, through him I got a job which protected me for a time from the roundups in the ghetto, which were becoming more and more frequent. On Serebrianski's recommendation, Hirsh Ruditzer sent me out to work as a boilerman in the ghetto hospital, where the metallurgist Haim Feigelman was employed. (He too had political reasons for keeping a low profile.) From that moment, the cellar became my home. Here I slept and ate my "meals" — the same rations that were served to the patients in the hospital. This was arranged by Dr. Leyb Kulik, the Director of the hospital.

I kept in constant touch with Notke Wainhoyz. From him I got the latest radio news about the real situation on the war fronts. These reports were fundamentally different from the "reliable" rumors that circulated through the ghetto about the continuing Soviet victories. There were refugees in the ghetto from cities and towns to the east of Minsk who assured us that "back there" the sound of cannon-fire and aerial bombardment was coming closer and closer, a sign that the battles were moving toward Minsk. There were even informants who, "with their own ears," had heard from a friendly peasant, who had brought a sack of potatoes to barter at the ghetto fence, that Soviet military reconnaissance units had recently been seen near his village.

These and similar reports, which one wag called "news from YIVO" (*Yidn Viln Azoy*, Jews want it that way) acted as a narcotic that helped people hold out against the incessant German roundups in the ghetto streets and during the terrible nights behind the barricaded doors of their houses. The ghetto even saw the birth of a new profession of news broadcasters. A friend of mine from Grodno boasted that with his fabricated "good news" he helped whole families — and himself at the same time. In every house into which he brought his good news from the fronts, he was given a "meal" and was even able to put aside a bit of extra bread "for later."

I discussed this with Notke and it was during this conversation that the answer to the question, "What is to be done?" came up for the first time. Utilizing Notke's radio reports about the true situation on the war-fronts (no matter how sad they were) we could fight against the illusion of the "imminent liberation." Jews must know what the truth was, they must find the strength to endure, not to live with the false conviction that their troubles would soon be over. Notke agreed to put together several pages of radio news from Moscow. For the work of copying and distributing this news I enlisted a group of people who lived in the little wooden house on Obutkova Street. They accepted my proposal as the first step in a program of "doing something." These were, first of all, my old friends Cesia Madeisker and Meir Feldman, who in turn recruited Ber Sarin (Moyshe Levin), his wife Sarah, and even a grey-haired neighbor of theirs who knew where there was an old typewriter.

The frequent reports from the front, despite the fact that they negated the fabricated "good news," did not lead to any evident mass depression. On the contrary, people who were listening to our reports soon began taking it as a sign that "our guys were here in the ghetto." People who went outside the ghetto to work reported that "they themselves saw" the former Minister of Education, Uralova, steal past them on the street. Others told about former Soviet leaders who had gotten themselves into various jobs "for the Germans" in order to do "a certain kind of work." These stories were always told in the most conspiratorial whispers.

Over the years, Soviet citizens had grown accustomed to receiving orders, directives, slogans — always from above. The rumors about Soviet officials who had stayed behind "to do underground work" raised the hopes of ghetto Jews that instructions would soon come from above as to what they should do "until our guys returned." The "afishkes," as Minsk Jews called the news bulletins that we pasted up inside the ghetto, served to confirm these rumors (which later proved to be utterly groundless). The Byelorussian Soviet leaders who ran away in such haste left no one at all behind in the occupied capital who could organize resistance against the enemy. But at that time this was not clear either in the ghetto or on the "other side," where some people (including former high Soviet army officers) began to meet and ask themselves "what is to be done?"

The answer to that question did not come from above; it had to come from the people themselves. Certainly this was true inside the ghetto. After the events of August 1941 most Jews began to realize that no one's life was now safe in the ghetto, that even "good jobs" and "good documents" were no guarantee against the murderous "brown raids."* Three times that month the ghetto was completely surrounded. On August 14, 25 and 31 the *Einsatzkommandos*, with the help of Lithuanian fascists, local police and specially trained dogs, carried out mass roundups of Jewish men. With beatings and

---

* So-called because the raids were conducted by "brown shirts," or Nazis.

[26]

savage yells thousands of prisoners were herded into Jubilee Square and from there deported to — where?

As a result, two new word-concepts became widespread among the ghetto Jews: Tutshinka and Shiroka. Before the war, Tutshinka was the headquarters of the Sixth Division of the NKVD in Minsk. Now the Germans turned it into a prison for the Jews captured during the August *actions** — men, women and children. One man who escaped from there reported that first they were all ordered to empty their pockets and undress. Then they were herded toward a freshly dug ditch, where machine-guns finished the hideous work. Some of the victims did not die immediately. The groans of the wounded could be heard all along the mass grave. The survivor found himself underneath a dead body. During the night he somehow managed to escape undetected and made his way to the ghetto. After he told his grisly story, Tutshinka became a synonym for mass murder, along with Trostinietz, the camp where the piles of corpses were incinerated.

"Shiroka" was the name given to the concentration camp inside Minsk itself. (It was located on Shiroka Street.) Some of the Jews captured in the August *action* were sent to that camp. It is not known why they in particular were selected. The head of "Shiroka" was S.S. *Sturmbannführer* Lokai. His assistant was the sadistic Lt. Gorodietski. We later learned that Gorodietski was descended from a Russian family that emigrated to Germany. For the captured Jews and for Judenrat members he had no other term of address but "you filthy *zhid-bolsheviks.***" And he punctuated his epithets with his rubber truncheon. Whenever Gorodietski appeared in the ghetto the Jews disappeared from the streets.

In those August days the word "melina" or "malina" (from criminal terminology) also became current. Without the slightest connection to other ghettos, where hiding in camouflaged places — cellars, attics, behind ovens, even in walls — arose everywhere as a means of defense against the Nazi attacks, Jews in the Minsk ghetto arrived at the same measures. People became extraordinarily inventive. One night, when I had to stay late at the one-room home of the Jewish metalworker Haim Zucker — a man who never succumbed to dejection and who was able in any situation to find a way out — he unexpectedly revealed to me a double wall where we would have hidden in the event of a sudden German raid.

For the first time in my meetings with Notke Wainhoyz in his attic "melina" we both came to the same conclusion: We must start doing some-

---

* German *aktion*, a euphemism for the raids in which Jews were rounded up for slave labor or death.

** Jewish Bolsheviks.

thing! To remain passive and helpless in the face of the Nazi death sentence that hung over us all would only make it easier for the "brown murderers" to carry out their plans. But what could we do?

We decided that the first step was to call together a number of trustworthy people and consider what the answer to that question might be. My own connections were with absolutely safe individuals, but none of them were local, they all came from "the west," and therefore had no broad contacts among the Jews of Minsk. Notke, who forewarned me that because of his situation it would be unwise for him to leave his hiding-place to attend the meeting, gave me two important things: suggestions about what we could begin to do, and names of several local people who, in his opinion, could be trusted implicitly. All of us were aware that we had to come to the meeting with well thought-out plans, because it was very risky to prolong the meeting beyond a certain time.

The meeting took place on the 17th of August, 1941 — the second ghetto month — a period when the threat of death-raids by Hitler's *Einsatzkommandos* hung constantly over the Jews of Minsk.

Conflict between "Westerners"
and "Easterners"

Through Notke Wainhoyz I met with two natives of Minsk — Boris Haimovitsh, who was a former director of a large textile factory and a reserve officer in the Red Army, and Isaiah Shnitman, a textile worker. Both men had many friends on "the other side" and both of them had heard that "something was happening." They agreed to come to the meeting and also promised to speak with others, to find out what they were thinking and to make certain decisions.

We chose a place which was so situated that we could get out easily in case of danger. It happened to be the home of Sonya Rivkin, a native of Leningrad, who had been with the Russian army on the western border and during the retreat had remained stuck in Minsk. The flat was on Ostrovski Street, near Jubilee Square, and not far from the Judenrat, which was now housed in the former headquarters of the Fourth Soviet military district on Ratomski Street. Because the neighborhood was always so busy, the people coming to the meeting would have a chance of getting to Sonya's place unnoticed.

We chose a Sunday when, as a rule, no German "actions" took place. Sonya's flat had the great virtue of three exits: Ostrovski Street, Republikaner Street and Hlebna Street. Sonya herself stood guard outside, along with several young women who had agreed to help. They would give us a signal in the event of trouble.

There were five of us at the meeting — two Minskers (Boris Haimovitsh and Isaiah Shnitman) — two "westerners" (Meir Feldman and myself) and Jacob Kirkaieshto, from Odessa, former Propaganda Secretary of the Bialystok Communist Party committee. Excused from attending were Notke Wainhoyz, Hirsh Dobin and Haim Aleksandrovitsh. (The last-named came from a well known proletarian family in Grodno.) I spoke with the three who did not attend, both before and after the meeting.

At the meeting I reported Notke's opinion. He proposed one single task:

[29]

to combat the illusions of the Jews in the ghetto about "waiting out" the war, protecting themselves in "good work-places." This would be done by word of mouth and by written propaganda. By that time there were already a good number of skilled workers in the ghetto who worked for the German airforce commissariat and other military services. They were marched in and out of the ghetto by German soldiers who had a kind of "proprietary" interest in them. They would not allow the police at the gates to search "their Jews" and often these soldiers traded with the ghetto, using their Jewish workers as go-betweens.

The purpose of Notke's proposals was to overcome the complete disorientation of the Jews in the Minsk ghetto with regard to German intentions toward Jews in general and to Soviet Jews in particular. This disorientation was particularly effective among the Jews because fresh in their minds was the idyllic relationship between the Soviet Union and Hitler Germany after the signing of the Molotov-Ribbentrop pact on August 23, 1939. They vividly recalled Molotov's mockery of the anti-Nazi fighters, whom he called "naive anti-fascists." It was Molotov who referred to German National-Socialism as "a matter of taste." Jews in the ghetto could not help but wonder: How did it happen that a week before the Hitler attack (June 14, 1941) an official communiqué of the Soviet Telegraphic Agency Tass denied categorically that Germany had any intentions of attacking the Soviet Union.

Notke proposed that the "westerners" prepare materials setting forth everything they knew — and which the Jews of Minsk did *not* know — about Hitler's pogroms in Germany and all the occupied countries. These materials would make clear that in regard to Soviet Jews, whom the Nazis called Bolsheviks, commissars and spies, the terror and the mass executions were already being carried out without interruption.

These proposals were accepted by all of us, but we did not agree that we should limit ourselves to explanations. Jews would certainly ask: "If all this is true, what are we doing to save ourselves?" And how would we reply to that?

We decided therefore that we had to do two things: (1) Spread these slogans among the population: "Ghetto means death! Break down the ghetto walls! Out of the ghetto!" (2) Send some of our people who looked "Aryan" into various neighborhoods to find places where Jews could hide and survive.

We all agreed, further, that in order to start "doing something" it would be necessary to set up an organizational center that would seek out trustworthy, determined individuals who could influence the ghetto population. The customary criterion for such people in Minsk was their prewar membership in the Communist Party or the Komsomol. In practice, however, this did not count for very much. Personal recommendation from the initiating group was enough to erase the distinction between Party and non-Party people. Furthermore, all the "westerners" were non-Party ever since the Comintern's decision to liquidate the Communist Parties of Poland, the Western Ukraine and Western Byelorussia as "nests for provocateurs." *No other political groupings existed in the Minsk ghetto.* There were, however, people of the older generation who had formerly belonged to the Bund (Jewish Labor Federation) or to various Zionist parties. These movements had no organized expression in the Minsk ghetto, but the individuals — because of their experiences in the early years of the Revolution — did have an influence when we came to consider the question of "what is to be done?"

Everyone agreed, also, that it was absolutely necessary to make contact with trustworthy Russians and Byelorussians "on the other side" to help us set up the conditions under which we could save people from death in the ghetto.

The following were chosen to be in the organizing center: (1) Jacob Kirkaieshto, responsible for setting up the technical means of conducting underground work — finding typewriters, radio sets (which were forbiddenin the ghetto), places to meet, and organizing a group of people to act as couriers; (2) Notke Wainhoyz, responsible for propaganda work, for writing the material to be distributed among the ghetto population; (3) Yefim, (that is, me) as secretary of the center. My main task was to build an organization based on cells of ten people; at the head of each cell would be trusted individuals who could make their own decisions in an emergency.

In the extraordinary conditions prevalent in the ghetto, the underground experience of the "westerners" in prewar Poland was extremely useful. The "easterners" hadn't the slightest idea of the elementary rules of illegal political work. We were thus faced with the danger that, even before we managed to do anything, the Gestapo would wipe out our people, thereby terrorizing the whole ghetto still further.

One of our decisions was that if any one of us fell into the hands of the Gestapo, we would try, at the first opportunity, to escape, even if it meant a bullet in the back, rather than risk the possibility of breaking under torture. This decision made a deep impression on our inner circle, young and old alike. Our people learned to live with the thought that the danger was real, that we must be careful of every word we said and every step we took, but that we must be ready, at the same time, to pay with our lives rather than be captured by the enemy.

With all this, we stressed the importance of not isolating ourselves from

[31]

the general population; we had to know what the mood was, what Jews were saying; we had to be thinking constantly of ways to influence them.

We saw the results of our efforts first among the young people, who as a general rule are more impassioned, more exuberant and more ready to reveal their thoughts and feelings. Two of the young people played an extraordinarily important part in the building of our organization. Zhenka, 17 years old, was the first to put us in touch with the "outside world." Emma, 18 years old, held all the internal organizational contacts in her hands. Both these young people had the same qualities — they were "born underground workers." Almost in military fashion they quickly understood and accepted directives that were given to them. Both of them were close-mouthed and rarely asked questions about the purpose of dangerous steps they were asked to take. They knew that a misstep could be fatal, but they considered their own personal fate secondary to the larger cause.

I met Zhenka through his father, Gertsik, who was the administrator of the ghetto hospital. He would often stop in to see me for a little chat in the boiler-room. He believed that we — the westerners — knew a lot more than they — the *"Sovetske."* One day, when we had gotten to know each other better, he confided to me that he felt very bad about his 17-year-old David, who was "living like a Gentile" on the other side and always carried a gun. Gertsik, his grey goatee bobbing up and down nervously, asked me if I would please have a talk with David the next time he was in the ghetto and try to persuade him to return to his parents. . .

From the conversation with David, who seemed to trust me, I learned that he was now called "Zhenka," that he was in touch with his school friends on the other side and that they had all pledged to fight against the Nazis in whatever way they could. They were in touch with some of the older people who felt the same way. I asked if he would set up a meeting for me with one of those older people. He said he would try, and would let me know. Blond, robust, broad-shouldered, jauntily dressed, he looked nothing at all like his emaciated father with the angular face. And unlike his father, Zhenka didn't say very much. Occasionally, to let me know that he understood what I was saying, he snapped the Soviet slang word *poryadek*, which signifies "everything will be arranged."

Emma Radova, a dark-haired, pretty young woman with piercing black eyes in a round face, I met about a month later. It happened this way. From several Jews I learned that while they were returning from work in a military installation they had seen twelve victims hanging on a gallows and that one of them was a young woman. The placard around her broken neck said: "We, Partisans, shot at German soldiers." The German guard who was leading the workers had burst out angrily: *"Diese ist eine Judin!"* (This one is a Jewish woman!)

Shortly thereafter, Zhenka told us that the girl was Masha Bruskin, 17 years old, a Jewish girl from Minsk. She had worked as a nurse in a hospital. We also learned that she was a cousin of the noted Jewish sculptor Z. Azgur, a member of the Soviet Academy of Arts. We found several young people in the ghetto who had been her schoolmates. In this way we met Emma Radova and Dora Berson, who had known Masha and who characterized her as a strong but romantic young woman who had been active in school affairs.

In the course of telling Masha's heroic story to more and more young people in the ghetto, resistance groups were formed among the youth in the ghetto, led by Emma and Dora. From time to time Zhenka (David Gertsik) gave them some help. (Years later, *Trud*, organ of the Soviet Trade Unions, published a lengthy article about Masha Bruskin — without mentioning that she was a Jew — in which the writer described how she went to the gallows. "This is not the way one goes to one's death — this is how one goes into eternity.")

Despite all our precautions, word did reach people that "something was happening," that the news reports from the front were not the whole story. (Notke Wainhoyz received these broadcasts by the "Soviet Information Bureau" with the help of Abraham Tunik, a radio technician.) Rumors circulated about contacts with "good Germans" who were helping Jews, about a truck that carried bread from the big bakery and that the German guards who escorted this truck were tossing loaves of bread to Jews on the street.

News of our existence reached a group of Jewish workers who met regularly in a room at #46 Republikaner Street, near the ghetto border on Niemiga Street. Through a friend of Sonya Rivkin they sent word that they wanted to meet with one of our representatives.

Thus it came about that I first met Nochem Feldman, the leader of the group, who had fought with the partisans in the Civil War. Short, stooped, with dark brown hair and grey temples, he was in his late forties, and his hardened face was covered with wrinkles. Listening to my "plain talk," he squinted his eyes and looked aside, as if he were highly skeptical of what he was hearing. When I proposed that he and I meet alone, so that I could tell him in confidence about our group and what it was doing, he replied sarcastically that all the people in the room were "kinfolk" from whom there were no secrets.

Then he introduced me to the others present: Getzl Oppenheim, a printer; Yeselevitsh, a shoemaker; Misha Tshiptshin, former technical director of the largest printing-house in Minsk; Velvl Losik, a worker in the

Kaganovitch factory; Lena Maiselis, a Party functionary; Zyama Okun, a government employee.

When I asked what they were planning to do, I got a vague answer about "we will do something. . . time will tell," etc. I believe this sort of talk was a result of their lack of trust in me. They weren't sure what kind of character I was, especially when they realized immediately from my "good Yiddish" that I was a "westerner." I told them candidly about our group, who we were, what we were doing, what we had already accomplished. They listened avidly, but the only question that Feldman asked me was more an accusation than a question:

"What do you mean you formed an organization? *Who gave you the right to do that?* Who gave you the order to form an organization?"

As far as the people in his group were concerned, they had formed no organization of any kind. The decisions they made affected their own personal fate, which they did have a right to do. They were all preparing to leave the ghetto, to try and reach a forest and fight as partisans, as they had done in 1919 and 1920.

"And what about the fate of all the other Jews?" I asked them. Their answer: "It's hopeless. . . There's a war on. . . If we had all been mobilized into the army at the beginning of the war, we wouldn't even have been able to do anything at all to protect our own families. . ."

My explanations about Hitler's program of total annihilation of the Jews, about all the horrible things that we had discovered during the eight years of Nazi rule, about the necessity of finding ways to rid the Jews of the illusion that they could "hold out" in the ghetto — all this they reacted to as if they were hearing it for the very first time.

In addition to weapons, the Feldman group had available to them a great deal of printing materials, which Kaplan and Misha Arotzker, both printers, were systematically taking out of the plant they worked in. Lena Maiselis was their contact person. They were doing this with the help of a Byelorussian named Podpriga.

They accepted the suggestion that, for the time being, they should use the printing materials for leaflets, news bulletins from the front, and for making false ghetto passports, work passes, and "Russian documents." We found a cellar on Ostrovski Street (#9) and Misha Tshiptshin was assigned to organize the first illegal print-shop in the occupied Byelorussian capital. (Misha Tshiptshin's name is mentioned in all the official archives and in the works of Soviet historians who wrote about the combat organization in Minsk, but in most cases there is no mention of the fact that it was the ghetto organization that planned and set up the shop and that the organizer was a Jew, a member of the combat organization in the ghetto.)

Shortly afterward, when I reported to Feldman that we were now also in touch with "the other side" and that "something was happening" there too, he understood it to mean that our organization had now been okayed "from above." Not until then did he tell us that his entire group and all their contacts would organize themselves into cells of ten, as parts of the over-all organization. We coopted Nochem Feldman into our organizational center, together with Zyama Okun, whom we empowered to join the ghetto police and recruit people there who would help us.

Feldman's certainty that we had received permission "from above" to form our organization was completely without foundation. On "the other side," with which we had begun to make some contacts, their attitude toward us was one of reserve, although it was we in the ghetto who had first demonstrated that it was not necessary to wait for "orders from above," that what was necessary first of all was to unite the various resistance groups into a single fighting organization. (This is touched on by Ivan Novikov in his book, *Ruins Shoot Straight*, as well as by the historian V. S. Davidova in the anthology, *Heroes of the Underground,* published in Moscow in 1970. It is also mentioned in *Legendary People*, Moscow, 1968.)

Our first meeting with "the other side" happened this way. Quite unexpectedly, Zhenka told me one day that I must go with him immediately to meet an important and trustworthy man on the other side. I barely managed to get myself ready. I borrowed Dr. Kulik's respectable-looking Russian blouse and before I knew it we were at the exit from the hospital. The guard — Lisa Riss, a member of one of our cells — sent her ten-year-old daughter Rita out to stand across the street and watch for police or Germans or any other suspicious persons. Little Rita did her job expertly, giving us the all-clear signal with her skinny little hand. We walked toward the cemetery, where there was a camouflaged hole in the wire fence — Zhenka's "door" into the ghetto.

After several months in the ghetto, a normal street looked strange to me, totally different from the ghetto streets, where fear clouded the face of every passerby, where tenseness and caution resulted in an unnatural, hurried, nervous gait. We were in a neighborhood that had suffered very little from the bombardments. The houses were one-story. The night was quiet and sleepy, as though nothing had happened here, as though people in the neighboring ghetto were not dying of starvation and all manner of sickness, were not sure of their lives either by day or by night.

[35]

My first impression upon coming into a clean room, with a neatly covered table in the center, was the surprised look on everyone's face, so different did *I* look, apparently, from a "normal" person on *their* side of the city. The first one to show me a friendly smile was a young man with the erect bearing of a professional soldier. Shaking my hand, he introduced himself with one word — "Slavek!" I responded in the same way — "Yefim!" Next to him stood a young woman with a warm, pleasant smile on her face. "My name is Lola." The owners of the flat, two elderly people, merely nodded their heads in greeting and went into the kitchen.

There wasn't an iota of doubt in my mind that the two people who had come to meet me deserved our full confidence and that we could talk openly with them. They wanted details about the situation in the ghetto, what were the people there thinking, and the main thing — "what kind of organization is it that you formed?"

I explained as fully as I could, emphasizing that we needed the help of the "Russian side" if we were to have any chance of saving ourselves. Then came Slavek's question. It was almost word-for-word the same as Nochem Feldman's: "From whom did the directive come to form your organization? Who assigned you the tasks that your group adopted as a program?"

My answer, which took them both by surprise, was a mute gesture — I pointed to my heart. And then I spoke what must have been the most remarkable words these young people had ever heard:

"Revolutionaries, who guide themselves solely by the interests of the people, must — in time of trouble, or under siege, or when they are completely isolated — listen to their own conscience. Under those circumstances, to wait for directives from above means to remain passive, powerless." When I told them that even in the concentration camps or in prison, people organize to fight for their lives, the look in their eyes was filled with so much curiosity and incredulity that it seemed I had just disclosed to them the most amazing fact in the world.

For a moment there was silence. Then came Slavek's worried question: "Well, good, let's say that we ourselves decide to go ahead and organize. What happens, however, if it turns out that there is already an underground organization in the city that has been empowered from above? Won't we look like usurpers who have taken upon themselves the right to organize, to lead an organization?"

I later learned that the answer I gave him was not completely persuasive. "If such an organizational center really does exist, then they'll find out about you only when you organize and start doing something. Then they'll find a way to contact you and take you under their wing." To illustrate this, I told him how we had found out about Feldman's group.

We took leave of each other most warmly, with the promise that Zhenka would put us in touch again.

Very soon after this I heard from Slavek that at a special meeting they had decided to form one central combat organization of all the separate groups in Minsk, especially the railroad workers, the government employees, various factory workers and intellectuals. The ghetto organization would be one of its components. Who would head the organization? "A supplementary committee." This was an expression of Slavek's fear that he might be accused of usurping the leadership, if it turned out that an underground Minsk leadership already existed.

A supplementary committee. That's what it was called at first. *Dopolnitielny komitet*. Heading this committee would be Slavek, who told me that he would use a pseudonym — *Pobiedit* ("to be victorious"). And I was given the pseudonym *Skromni*. I felt very uncomfortable with this. For decades I had given myself various pseudonyms. My own mother, in her letters, called me "Henia," a woman's name, for security reasons. And here he decrees a pseudonym for me in which I call myself by the immodest name of *"Skromni"* — which means "the modest one." But I couldn't do anything about it.

In his book, Ivan Novikov tells the story behind this strange name. At the first meeting of his group, Slavek reported that he had met a representative of the ghetto organization who had really been sent by the Comintern! Apparently my arguments about combat groups in prisons and camps had led Slavek and Lola to such a conclusion.

When I told Dr. Kulik about the meeting with Slavek he hugged me and whispered emotionally, "Maybe — maybe there's a way out. . . "

At the "home" of Meirke Feldman and Cesia Madeisker, together with Ber Sarin and Sarah Levin, we relaxed with half a liter of Samogon vodka. I returned to my boiler-room greatly encouraged and deeply moved by the concern that Lisa, the guard, had shown me at the hospital gate:

"Be careful, Yefim, don't travel around too much. . . "

After the Great Provocation

"As long as I am alive I shall not fall into the hands of the enemy."
This pledge was fulfilled first by Jacob (Jascha) Kirkaieshto. In the ghetto environment, which was completely strange to him, he had displayed admirable organizational skills in devising methods that are indispensable for underground political work. He and I often used to talk about the "old days." We had formed a special relationship because I knew the place in Odessa where he had grown up. Orphaned during the pogrom years of 1919-20, he had been "adopted" by the Home for Jewish Workers' Children, which was maintained by YIDGEZKOM *(Yiddisher Geselshaftlekher Komitet)*, with the help of the Joint Distribution Committee. I had even given a few lectures there.

One day, Gorodietski and his thugs came into the ghetto to hunt Jews. At that same moment, Jascha left his "melina" to meet with one of our members. Gorodietski approached him with his automatic drawn. Jascha ran, zigzagging. One of the bullets from Gorodietski's gun lodged in his heart.

So far as I know, the funeral for Jacob Kirkaieshto was the only one ever held in the ghetto. And in violation of all the rules of illegal organization, scores of members of our cells attended his quiet burial. The little board on his grave said simply that he had "fallen in battle."

In the cemetery that day, Zyama Okun (who had joined the Jewish police) introduced me to a middle-aged man who later played a major role in both the ghetto organization and the all-Minsk combat center. His name was Michel (Misha) Gebelev. At first, Gebelev listened rather skeptically to all my talk about "what was going to happen next." His eyes lowered, he did not respond with so much as a word. But what Misha represented — his thorough familiarity with the city, with all its various neighborhoods, and most important, his long friendship with many people "on the other side" as a Party leader — this was for us an unparalleled opportunity to establish ties outside the ghetto.

Misha Gebelev thus became a member of our organizational center in place of Jacob Kirkaieshto. He and I too became the best of friends. And even though, in our conversations about the ghetto, he seemed to be always hopeless and pessimistic, there was no one like him when it came to getting things done. For him there was no difference between day and night. He was always ready. He had made a special "exit" for himself in the fence on Novo-Miasnitzka Street. There he had hidden a jacket without yellow patches and a carpenter's tool-box, his "cover." At that particular spot on the other side of the fence there was no regular police guard. Misha used to "cross the border" there at the oddest hours. He maintained regular contact with Slavek and helped the general combat center make new contacts throughout the city.

The truth is, he did take too many chances, and we often scolded him for this in no uncertain terms. He would listen patiently, his sad eyes downcast, with an occasional snort of his nose, and say nothing. His contact in the "Russian zone," Clara Zelesniak, called him "Herman the Fearless." Anya, another one of his contacts (I never knew her last name), called him "The Flying Dutchman." Misha, however, never acted as though he were doing anything out of the ordinary.

Until —

Until the 7th of November, 1941, the anniversary of the Revolution, when the Nazis staged their great provocation. This anniversary — *Oktiabrske*, as the Jews called it — had become a popular custom among Soviet citizens, who no longer observed the traditional ethnic holidays at all, or else did so in the privacy of their homes. This was especially true of the religious aspects of the holidays. But everyone in the ghetto remembered this holiday. Women would ask each other: "What are you baking for *Oktiabrske*?" and the bitter answer would be, "Chills and fever, seasoned with heartache."

Genia, the head nurse at the hospital, who knew of my friendship with Dr. Kulik, the director, asked his permission to put aside a bit of whiskey for making a drink in honor of *Oktiabrske*. I was invited to celebrate the holiday at the home of Ida Aler, a working-woman on Opanski Street. From things that I said, Ida had concluded that I was "kinfolk." She and her two daughters belonged to one of our cells.

A few days earlier, Zyama Serebrianski, chief of the ghetto police, had suddenly appeared in the boiler-room. In a festive, hail-fellow-well-met fashion he asked Haim Feigelman, the foreman, how the work was going. All this time he hadn't even looked in my direction. And as if explaining the reason for his visit, he said, "We'll see what can be done about helping the hospital." Then he caught my eye — he wanted to talk to me. When he left, I followed him. My first thought was that someone had "blown my cover."

When he told me, however, that Notke Wainhoyz had sent him, everything became clear.

The fate of thousands of Jews was at stake. Something had to be done quickly. Zyama had learned from a reliable source that the Germans were getting ready to "cut off" a whole area of the ghetto which included Niemiga, Ostrovski and other densely populated streets. Zyama calculated that almost 20,000 Jews lived there. Where would we find homes for them all? Neither Zyama nor I realized at that moment what "cutting off" streets from the ghetto actually portended. It never occurred to us that it meant more than merely reducing the geographical area. Our thoughts went in only one direction: to give the people in that neighborhood sufficient warning, so that they could move out in time.

In whispers, Zyama suggested that I meet with the head of the Judenrat. We could trust him — he had already put 2 and 2 together and assumed that there was "another authority" inside the ghetto. I categorically refused to meet with him. It would not be good for him and it would not be good for us. In Judenrat circles there were undoubtedly "eavesdroppers" who reported everything they heard to the Gestapo. The risk of failure was too great. I proposed instead that "people from the city" — not Jews — should establish direct communication with Zyama and perhaps also with Mushkin, the chairman of the Judenrat. Subsequently I had an opportunity to discuss this with Slavek personally.

When we heard the news about the reduction of the ghetto, our center instructed all the secretaries of the cells — by that time we had ten of them, not counting the youth groups — to mobilize their people and very quietly and circumspectly to warn the Jews in the danger-zone that they must find a place to move to before the Germans came to "evict" them. In many instances our people were greeted with despair and even resignation — "whatever will be will be." The younger people, however, listened.

It happened that I was responsible for warning Liza Voshtshulska, a member of my own cell. She lived on Niemiga, close to the ghetto border. Her flat had served as a meeting place with Emma Radova. Liza's 12-year-old son Vova was one of our swiftest "scouts" on the other side — even outside of Minsk — in finding safe places to hide. Tested in suffering and struggle, Liza heard me out without a word. She merely pointed to her old and lame mother and I knew she would never move from that place. . .

On the evening of November 6, 1941, when Gorodietski invaded the ghetto — it was at the hour when the work-groups were coming back — the streets instantly emptied out. That same evening we learned that Gorodietski had rounded up the Judenrat members and their families, the leaders of the ghetto police and the labor exchange, as well as several hundred "specialists" and skilled workers, and taken them all to the Shiroka concentration camp.

A great fear fell upon the ghetto population. No one slept that night. They had a premonition that the morning would bring with it a disaster. If the Germans had rounded up the leaders of the ghetto itself, then there would soon be no ghetto either.

On the morning of the 7th a detachment of S.S. and police, along with a large number of local and Lithuanian fascists, marched into the ghetto. They stopped at Jubilee Square. Then, concentrating on the streets around Niemiga and Ostrovski, they began "searching and seizing" men, women and children and herding them into Jubilee Square under a hail of blows and curses. The old and the feeble were shot on the spot. The Square and the surrounding streets filled up with people whose faces expressed only fear and despair.

Then came an order that was translated into Russian by the police from "the other side" (they were called "grave-diggers" because of their black uniforms):

"Line up in rows of eight, as you always do on Oktiabrske!"

People began pushing, dragging their children, trying to keep their families together. The Lithuanian fascists distributed large red flags bearing Soviet emblems. Into the hands of the men in the front row they stuck a banner:

"Long live the 24th anniversary of the Great Socialist October Revolution!"

From the Judenrat building nearby came groups of men in civilian clothing, carrying huge movie cameras. From all angles they filmed the "demonstration," as they ordered the Jews to smile and look happy, to put their children on their shoulders and start marching. The march went along Opanski Street, where a long line of black trucks was waiting. The police ordered the Jews to climb into the trucks, which then started moving toward Tutshinka Street. . .

Only a few people survived. From them we learned what had happened. The Germans forced everyone into the storehouses of the former Sixth NKVD Division. People lost consciousness but did not fall, because the bodies were so closely pressed together. Children suffocated. Thirst tortured all those still alive. For two or three days the Nazis kept the people standing in there. At the end of that time, the living were driven toward freshly dug ditches and ordered to undress. The screams of pain and terror and the curses of the guards drowned out the rattle of the machine-guns.

[41]

Then — silence. The bloody graves were left uncovered. For a long time the groans of people still accidentally alive could be heard. Peasants from a nearby village, who were brought in to cover the graves, reported that even after they covered them, the earth still moved. . .

The following day, the Judenrat members and all the others who had been taken hostage with them were brought back into the ghetto. The Germans explained to them that they had been removed from the ghetto for their own protection, so that they should not accidentally become victims of the massacre!

According to information available to the Judenrat, 12,000 Jews were killed on that day. There was no consolation in the fact that almost half the inhabitants of the "severed" neighborhoods had managed to save themselves because we had forewarned them.

But even before people could recover from the shock, the S.S. and the police again attacked the ghetto, assisted by their Lithuanian confederates. It was two weeks after the *Oktiabrske* massacre. This time they attacked the Tatarski Street neighborhood, the Jewish part of Zamkova Street and surrounding streets. The aim of the Germans was becoming clear: reduce the area of the ghetto on all sides, press the Jews closer and closer together, moving steadily in the direction of the cemetery.

Zyama Serebrianski informed me that during this "action" the Nazis came upon Notke Wainhoyz's hiding-place. No other details about Notke's death ever reached us. We had lost the man who, from his "malina" (hiding place), had managed to speak to and convince thousands of Jews not to despair, who had told them the unadorned truth about their situation and what they could expect in the future. We made no decisions without consulting Notke first; we counted on his basic knowledge of the character of Soviet Jews. When we broke our isolation and made contact with "the other side" it made him very happy.

Notke's death depressed us, but we were cheered a little by a note from Slavek proposing that we delegate someone to attend an urgent meeting of his group. We chose Misha Gebelev, who could move about more freely on the Russian side. We knew that he would be able to make a sound judgment about the participants in that meeting. We empowered him to bring them up to date about our situation and to ask for their help, first of all, in saving the women and children by finding places for them to live outside the ghetto. As far as the men were concerned, we asked that in all their plans to resist the Nazis, the organizational center should always keep our people in mind, especially those with military experience. By that time we had already heard reports of partisan groups, of entire detachments, particularly east of Minsk.

We suggested to Misha that he try to find out whether Slavek was prepared to come to the ghetto to meet with our center.

The taciturn Misha with the sad eyes came back this time a completely different man. What had taken place at #5 Lugowaia Street was not merely a meeting but an all-Minsk conference which had decided to unite all the combat groups, and there were many of them. They had adopted our organizational principle of "tens" and they had elected a "triumvirate" headed by Slavek-Pobiedit to carry on the work and to establish contact with partisans in the forest. We in the ghetto were made responsible for organizing an apparatus to do the printing of various materials for all the underground groups. (One of the rare documents found after the war contains the minutes of the first meeting of the "supplementary committee" which assigned this task to the secretary of the ghetto center, Comrade Skromni). Misha reported to us that Slavek was ready to come into the ghetto and consult with us on everything.

In the meantime we gave Nina Liss, who looked like a blonde, blue-eyed Byelorussian, the difficult task of going into the forest at the former Soviet-Polish border to ascertain whether we could settle some of our women and children there. We planned to provide them all with "good" documents. Nina's five-year-old daughter remained with her grandmother, with whom I had many long conversations in my free time.

Nina's mother had been wounded by a German bullet in the first days of the ghetto. It was difficult for her to walk, though she was still an energetic, exuberant woman. She accepted the task we had set for her daughter as if she herself were going to carry it out. More than once I heard her exclaim, "Come on, gang, show them what you can do!" Up until the 1920s she had been a Bundist. I never tired of her stories about the *skhudki* (strikes) and the *zabastovki* (illegal meetings) in which she had taken part. As a young working-woman she had also belonged to the Jewish Self-Defense during the first Russian Revolution. In the Bronislaw-Groser battalion, which was formed in 1919 to fight against the counterrevolutionary pogromchiks, she had served as a nurse. "What did you expect me to do — sit at home with my hands folded? If one must fall, it's better to fall in battle!" This brave, elderly woman had no way of knowing how soon she would fall, together with her heroic daughter and her only grandchild.

We set up a special apparatus to produce forged documents — workpasses with the Nazi eagle and "Aryan" passports. This was the responsibility of Ber Sarin, a master "copyist," and two members of Feldman's cell — Motya Sherman and Genia Kaplan — with the help of Soloveitshik, a former press photographer, a group that performed miracles in transforming

Jewish faces into Aryan ones. For mass-producing the forged passes we used the real blank forms supplied to us by workers in the print-shop that published the newspaper of the German military staff on the "middle" front.

(A report from *Einsatzkommando* A, dated 10/16/41 to 1/31/42, says that "one of the many organizations producing forged passports existed even in the municipal kommissariat"; cited by A. M. Ignatenko in Istorial KPSS, July 1975. That was true. At that time the Gestapo did not yet know about the mass production of all sorts of forged documents in our ghetto print-shop.)

At one point this activity helped us block the Nazi decree that would have divided the ghetto in two — which they planned to do by moving all workers with specialist passes (along with Judenrat members and leaders of the Jewish police) from Jubilee Square toward Obutkova Street, and all other Jews in the opposite direction. The purpose of this "reorganization" was now clear to everyone. The ghetto fell into a panic. People besieged the Labor Office demanding work as "specialists." We printed and distributed a large number of forged specialist passes. The officials of the Housing Section of the Judenrat then provided the German commandant of the ghetto with figures showing that in the area where specialists were permitted to live, there was no more room to settle all the workers carrying "German" passes. The commandant then decided that specialists could live in both parts of the ghetto.

For a while this resulted in calming the situation, though there was not a single calm day in the Minsk ghetto. There was not a day without murders, without brutality and terror, without the robbing of Jewish workers who had brought a little food back with them from the other side.

What was to be done? What was to be done?

New plans were made.

Two Authorities in the Ghetto

In their daily lives the Jews in the ghetto saw and felt the terrorizing German authority, which sowed death at every step. Inside the ghetto they saw (and wherever possible avoided) the ever-present chief of the German police and security forces, Gattenbach. His constant companion was a wolfhound who was ever ready, at his master's command, to pounce on fleeing Jews, including small children, who had already learned to "make tracks" as soon as that coldblooded murderer came into view.

Gattenbach used to show up in various parts of the ghetto, looking for his daily quota of women to beat because they were trying to trade some article or other at the fence for a few potatoes. He derived special pleasure from abusing children who had not managed to disappear from the street in time, or from tormenting old men who did not doff their hats to him quickly enough. Wintertime this was particularly difficult for them to do, because they had to untie the scarf that protected their ears from the cold. Very often he would drop a Jew like that with one bullet.

The German who used to "relieve" Gattenbach in the ghetto did his work a little more calmly and efficiently. His name was Richter and he was an older, more experienced Prussian police official who simply carried out the orders of his superiors. His brutality was unconcealed during the many "looting actions" which robbed Jews of their last possessions that might have served to keep them alive a little longer.

The winter of 1942 was exceptionally cold and there was no fuel to heat the ghetto buildings. Early in the evening, after Richter had finished his "tour of duty," people would saw down one of the remaining trees and divide it among the neighbors. Not a splinter was left of the doors and windows in the houses that were destroyed during the bombing of Minsk. Not a trace was left of the balconies in the nearby gardens. Everything was used for cooking or to protect oneself from the brutal cold. There was a saying in the ghetto: "Troubles as plentiful as wood, but nothing to burn." People burned up the outhouses in the courtyards. For their bodily functions they used the bit of open space alongside the buildings. While the weather was cold it wasn't so bad, but as soon as the weather turned a little milder the stench spread all through the ghetto.

This situation gave Richter another excuse to bare his claws. Mercilessly he beat anyone caught sawing down a tree or knocking down an outhouse or bringing back from the Russian zone a few sticks of wood or some sawdust or coals. His specialty: inspecting Jews who were returning from work, dumping the food out of their pockets, leaving it on the ground for the Jewish police to sort out and take whatever they could use.

Richter was eventually replaced by Benetzke, and after him, S.S. *Scharführer* Ribe, who was even more sadistic than his predecessors. Jews who had escaped from Slutzk and settled in the Minsk ghetto recognized him as the murderer who had been in charge of liquidating the Slutzk ghetto.

People called him "the Devil with the White Eyes." He was always accompanied by his translator, Michelson. Ribe never let any Jew he encountered go unscathed, regardless of age or sex. He would look at his victim with his big bulging eyes, his lips would form a smile, he would carefully aim his pistol — and never miss. It was Ribe who organized the "beauty contest" of young Jewish women, selected twelve of the youngest and prettiest, and ordered them to parade through the ghetto until they reached the Jewish cemetery. Here he forced them to undress and then shot them one by one. The last woman to be killed was Lena Neu. He took her brassiere from her and said smugly, "This will be my souvenir of the pretty Jewess." What did it matter to him that the Jew who had been brought along to cover the grave could hear him say it.

These satraps from the lower echelons of the S.S. were the daily, direct overseers of the ghetto. Their superior was Commandant Redder, about whom the ghetto population knew very little, except that he issued all the decrees against them. Redder would usually burst into Mushkin's room, chase everyone else out with his whip in a cruelly degrading manner and give his orders to Mushkin — whom he always called "You, head of the Jewish rabble!" And his orders were highly specific: so much and so much gold, so much and so much silver, so much and so much platinum — to be turned over not later than this-and-that date. All the Judenrat members were responsible for this with their lives. Within such and such a time all the furs — women's coats, men's coats, fur hats, collars, gloves — all must be turned in to the Commandant's office. From Redder came the order to surrender all watches, brass door knobs, copper pans. There was no end to the Commandant's inventiveness.

A special organ of terror was the murder squad of the Shiroka concentration camp, headed by Deputy Commandant Gorodietski. The sudden raids of these savage bandits always ended with the random murder of some Jews and the deportation of many others who were rounded up ostensibly for work but actually to fill the "quota" of bodies for burning at Trostynietz. The camp on Shiroka Street was under the direct supervision of the *Sicherheitsdienst* (Security Service), of which *Obersturmführer* Lokai was a member.

The entire system of terror in Byelorussia, particularly in Minsk, was headed by S.S.-and-Police General Zenner. (I carried a document with his forged signature, forbidding anyone to "recruit" me for forced labor without his knowledge and permission.) After February 1942, Zenner was replaced by *Obersturmbannführer* Edouard Strauch, head of the Security Service in Byelorussia, who had been sent from Berlin.

The ghetto population had only the barest notion of this whole system, the hierarchy and the competencies of the various parts of the terror apparatus. Even for the Judenrat it was difficult to keep track of all the rungs in this ladder of officials who kept giving them orders "over the head" of Commandant Redder. Attempts by Mushkin to explain that a previous decree had already confiscated the "requisitioned" property would often end with a blow to the head of this "Eldest of the Jews" himself.

The Judenrat did, however, sense a certain difference in the attitude of the civil administration that was set up in the early months of the occupation of Minsk in place of the Military Field Commander.

Ilya Mushkin had permission to leave the ghetto once a week, accompanied by one of the Judenrat members, for the purpose of obtaining the designated number of food products at the *uprava*, the "city hall." The norm determined by the German authorities for Jews — one-tenth the calories received by an Aryan — consisted primarily of cornmeal, some kasha, sometimes soap and medicines to combat typhus. (The Germans were deathly afraid of a typhoid epidemic.) At the head of the *uprava* were people unknown in Minsk, but it happened that I knew who those collaborators were: Dr. Tumash and Waclew Iwanowski. (More about that in a later chapter.)

At the head of the civil administration of occupied Byelorussia, which carried out the Hitler policy toward the Jews, was a General Kommissar. He was one of the first organizers of Hitler's National Socialist Party — the Gauleiter Wilhelm Kube. Son of a Prussian junior officer, he was already a deputy in the Reichstag as early as 1924, representing the ultra-right. In 1928 Kube headed the Nazi fraction in the Prussian legislature. At every opportunity he had demonstrated his anti-Semitic position. In a 1935 article, *On the Jewish Question*, in the West German *Beobachter* he wrote: "What plague or tuberculosis or syphilis means for the health of humanity, Jewry means for the way of life of the white races. . . . The carrier of this disease must be isolated and eliminated."

The General Kommissar of Byelorussia was subordinate to the *Reichskommissar* over the occupied territories, Heinrich Lohse, whose residence was in Riga. Lohse, in turn, was directly responsible to the Minister for the Occupied Territories, Alfred Rosenberg, who, from his office in Berlin determined the direction of the Hitler policy on the territory occupied during the blitzkrieg against the Soviet Union in 1941. Rosenberg's deputy Lohse was the "boss" of the General Kommissars over Ukrainia, Byelorussia, Lithuania and Estonia, all of them appointed by Berlin.

Wilhelm Kube's residence was on Freiheit Square in Minsk, in the buildings formerly occupied by the offices of the Soviet trade unions. (In the 1920s this square was chosen as the site for a monument to Hirsh Leckert, the Jewish labor martyr. For many years the base of the monument stood there, but the monument was never erected upon it.)

The General Kommissar over Byelorussia, like the General Kommissars over all the occupied territories, was concerned with ways to use material goods and labor power for the benefit of the Wehrmacht and the war economy of Nazi Germany. Wilhelm Kube devoted a great deal of attention to policy regarding museums, galleries, scientific institutions and cultural treasures. Scientific items, ancient documents, printed materials and paintings in particular were selected by a group of Nazi specialists and shipped to Germany. These specialists from Rosenberg's staff were also interested in Jewish archives, Jewish folklore and historical material in the former Institute of Jewish Culture at the Byelorussian Academy of Science. Through the Judenrat they tried to obtain Jewish co-workers.

Zyama Serebrianski suggested to me that if I agreed to work there I would receive an ironclad pass that would protect me against roundups and that I would be well provided with food. I rejected the offer and advised him not to try to find any other candidates. Apparently Rosenberg's office did find such people, because "The Eagle of the East," organ of the German "Middle" front, published examples of rhymed Yiddish folklore praising Stalin.
. . .

The Judenrat people felt, rather than knew, that between General Kommissar Kube, the civil authority, and *Obersturmbannführer* Strauch, the police authority, there were certain contradictions and differences in attitude toward the ghetto. This was expressed primarily in the relationship with "the ghetto within the ghetto" — the Jews who were brought to Minsk from Germany, Austria and Czechoslovakia after the November pogroms and settled in the houses vacated by the Soviet Jews who were taken out and murdered. ("I made room for you by getting rid of 35,000 Russian Jews," boasted *Oberscharführer* Scheidel to the German Jews who were deported to Minsk. Scheidel was the overseer of the S.S. and police in the ghetto of the "Hamburg" Jews. They were called by that name because the very first transport had come from Hamburg.)

Soon after their arrival the German Jews began building a fence to separate themselves from the Ostjuden. The Jews of Minsk, for the first time, saw Jews who had the same mannerisms as the Germans. While they were erecting the fence around their ghetto, they kept shouting orders about the work in exactly the same way as the German supervisors did to our Jews. They cleaned up the apartments, put things in order, began digging small plots of ground around the fences for vegetable gardens. After work every day they changed into "proper attire" for the evening.

The first contacts between them and the Minsk Jews were a result of the internal ghetto barter. The most sought-after food product for the "Hamburgs" was fat (*shpek*). They even established a schedule of prices. For one wristwatch — a pound of *shpek* and a loaf of bread, or a pound of margarine and two breads. The products that the "Hamburgs" received from the German authorities were enough only to cook a watery soup. (300 grams of water and 5 grams of kasha per person, with no fat or salt.) In order to quell their hunger, people traded their clothing, underwear, anything that had value "on the market."

This "business" soon attracted birds of prey — the "Black Police" from the Russian zone and our own Jewish police. There were also victims. *Obersturmführer* Birkhardt suddenly appeared in the "Hamburg" ghetto one day and emptied his automatic into a group of traders. Seven German Jews lay dead. And yet . . . half-an-hour later, in the shadow of death, this barter-trade was going on again. (See the testimony of Karl Lewenstein, a surviving chief of Jewish police in the Hamburg ghetto.)

Inside the Hamburg ghetto the Jews organized themselves according to the cities from which they had been deported. The *Juden-Altester* (The Jewish Elder) was Dr. Edgar Frank. The leaders of this ghetto of German Jews had no relationship with the Minsk Judenrat. Only once did they invite several Judenrat members, a special occasion on which they served them *latkes* (potato pancakes) made out of potato skins. At first the attitude of the "Hamburgs" toward the German civil administration was different than toward the Jews of Minsk. With the Germans they acted almost as fellow countrymen.

Toward the end of 1941 General Kommissar Kube visited the Hamburg ghetto and spoke with Dr. Frank, who reported to him that among the Jews

[49]

deported from Germany to Minsk were people "whose brothers were at the front" and that the *Ordnungsdienst* (police service) in the Hamburg ghetto consisted of men who had served in the German military during World War I, some of them of high rank and with medals of distinction. As Karl Lewenstein relates, General Kube was so impressed that he promised to transmit the information immediately to Adolf Hitler himself . . .

This relationship of Kube with the Hamburg ghetto gave rise to a conflict between the civil authority and the security organs. S.S. Chief Strauch complained to *Reichskommissar* Lohse in Riga, as well as to Rosenberg's Ministry of the Occupied Territories, that Wilhelm Kube had referred to the German Jews as "people of our own cultural sphere" and averred that "Mendelssohn could not be expunged from German cultural history." (Documents at Yad Vashem in Jerusalem.)

In one of his reports, Strauch characterized Kube as "incredibly opposed to actions against these Jews" and that "he limits the extermination actions to Polish and Russian Jews only." Strauch warned that the *Ordnungsdienst* of the German Jews was a well organized group of trained soldiers and that Kube stood in the way of their "special treatment" — that is, their liquidation. According to Strauch's report, after learning that the *Einsatzkommandos* had shot people in the ghetto of the Soviet Jews and left them lying in the street, Kube complained that "this does not befit the Germany of Goethe and Kant."

These denunciations, as well as Kube's response to them, reflected a conflict of competencies. The typical Nazi bureaucrat, Kube occasionally opposed Strauch because he prevented him from implementing certain plans to create organizations and agencies made up of Byelorussian collaborators. Thus, Strauch ordered the arrest and execution of Father Godlevski, a well known prewar Christian Democratic leader in Vilna, who took seriously Kube's promise about a future Byelorussian state within the framework of the Third Reich.

Most important, however, Strauch got in the way of Gauleiter Kube's policy on the German Jews. For a time the bloodthirsty Strauch had to reckon with an order from Berlin to refrain from any further *actions* that would affect the Jewish skilled workers in military workshops, or those who worked for the S.S. in the *Todt** organization. Fourteen hundred Minsk Jews worked in the railroad administration and several hundred in military installations. A report by *Einsatz* group A emphasized that in this area the

---

* A construction company for German defense installations outside of Germany.

Jews represented a high percentage of skilled workers "whom we cannot do without." (Yad Vashem, Document #2273).

This situation resulted in a secret circular (#220-41) sent by the Hitler government in Berlin, on December 3, 1941, simultaneously to the *Reichskommissar* of Ostland, the senior leaders of the S.S. and Police in Riga, the General Kommissars in Reval, Riga, Kovno and Minsk, and to the Commander of the Wehrmacht in Ostland. The circular states that according to the superintendent in the office of the Wehrmacht Commander in Ostland, Jewish skilled workers employed in arms factories and in renovation shops — who cannot for the time being be replaced — should not be listed for liquidation. The same applied also to Jewish skilled workers in factories not working directly for the German army but which were important to the war effort.

The Jews in the Minsk ghetto sensed a definite difference in the attitude of the civil authority as contrasted to the repeated raids by the *Einsatzkommandos* who systematically seized, murdered and thus reduced the number of Jews in the ghetto. Most ominous was the order creating two separate zones in the ghetto — one for craftsmen and skilled workers (also Judenrat members, Jewish police and related services) who carried passes issued by the German authority, the other (a much larger area) for the rest of the Jews. This order resulted in a state of panic among the ghetto population.

The "Hamburg" Jews were never subjected to any selections, although there were very few craftsmen among them; mostly they were middle-class people. The majority were put to work in military or war-production installations. The rest — as "people of our own cultural circle" — were helped for a time by the General Kommissar himself, who set up a special factory for the production of wagons. The idea was that, in the conditions then prevailing on the eastern front, the German army needed horse-drawn equipment. Some four hundred German Jews were employed (and temporarily saved) in this particular plant.

For a brief period after the order sparing the Jewish skilled workers, the roundups by the *Einsatzkommandos* and Gorodietski's camp-bandits ceased. However, judging from the whispered news that one could hear at the labor exchange before the German supervisors came to work, increasing numbers of Jews were being murdered in their homes during the night. For these victims, no "protective document" was of any use. On this "front" Kube's civil authority and the SS were in complete agreement.

They had discovered the activity of the Jewish Combat Organization.

Between Powerlessness and Power
in the Ghetto Itself

How many Jews were left in the Minsk ghetto after the German "actions" in the last months of 1941? According to the Judenrat, up to that date more than 30,000 Jews — men, women and children — had been taken away. After this bloody harvest, how many Jews were left in the ghetto? On first hearing, the answer to that question was hard to believe. According to the Judenrat figures there were still 80,000 people in the ghetto in December 1941 — just as many as when the ghetto was first set up.

How was that possible?

The truth is that as early as the second month in the ghetto the number of Jews there was estimated at more than 100,000. No one knew the exact figure, but the unexpectedly large number at the beginning of 1942 was due to the destruction of all the Jewish communities in the towns around Minsk by the *Einsatzkommandos*. Some Jews from those places managed to flee to Minsk. A certain number of skilled workers were brought to Minsk by the Germans themselves. Around that same time the houses that were left vacant after the German raids were occupied by the "Hamburg" Jews. Minsk became a central point for Jews deported from the German Reich.

From our people who worked on the railroad we learned about whole transports of German Jews that were halted and guarded only lightly for days at a time. Recognizing the Minsk Jews by their yellow patches (the German Jews wore yellow Stars of David with the word "*Jude*"), people in the trains began to beg for water and food. The German guards, of course, allowed no one to come anywhere near the trains. A member of our underground, however, did succeed in getting close enough to shout a warning to the Jews inside that they were being taken to their death and that they should try to escape. But where to? With young children, with old parents, with no knowledge of the language . . .

We now have documentary evidence that both the civil and the security authorities in Minsk appealed to Riga and Berlin not to send any more Jews from "the Reich" to the overcrowded Minsk ghetto. Simultaneously with the arrival of thousands of German Jews, the killing of Minsk Jews was intensified, thus "freeing" their apartments.

The only public address to which the ghetto Jews could take their troubles was the Judenrat. People would run there weeping and lamenting whenever the police caught a child who had crossed over to the Russian side to buy food for his starving family. People would come with money that they had been hiding, or with valuables that the Judenrat might use to free an arrested son or husband. It was rumored that the Judenrat was able to ransom prisoners. And there actually were such instances. Judenrat member Ruditzer was in touch with the warden of the Minsk prison, an ethnic German named Ginter. For a large sum of money he released a few prisoners, but this was possible only when the arrested Jews had not yet been interrogated by the Gestapo.

In general we felt the powerlessness of the Judenrat. All they could do for Jews whose family members were caught in a Nazi raid was to comfort them with the lie that the prisoners were being sent "somewhere to work." The disappointment that soon followed when the few survivors of the Trostynietz massacres came back to the ghetto grew into a hatred of those liars, the members of the Judenrat.

This hatred was demonstrated openly by the steadily increasing number of hungry people who besieged the Judenrat offices as soon as the work groups left the ghetto in the morning. Covered in rags, their faces swollen from cold and malnutrition, they would break into the offices and assault the staff. The Social Assistance section, which distributed food to the Children's Home, the hospital and the soup kitchen, began to "put aside" certain things for a number of needy people in order to "turn away their wrath." The Judenrat also helped the poorest of the poor with shoes and clothing left by victims of the Germans. On recommendation from the Social Assistance section, the people in the Labor Office tried to send the poorest people out to jobs where the workers were served meals.

All the same, the Judenrat continued to arouse the animosity of the population. Its members — among them some well known cultural and artistic figures — were accused of corruption, of "skimming off the cream" for themselves and their friends. The hatred mounted to a peak whenever the Judenrat, but primarily the *Ordnungsdienst* (on German orders), confiscated valuables from the ghetto population. The Jewish police went from house to house conducting thorough searches in which they often uncovered hiding-places and confiscated everything that people had been keeping to exchange for food. In some cases the searchers took things that were not even "on the list." Any attempt to resist was met by threats to report this hidden "property" to the "right places."

The issue of the Judenrat and the Jewish police gave rise to an internal conflict between us in the ghetto and the general Minsk resistance center. Up to that time there was a widespread feeling among the Jews that in addition to the despised and largely powerless Judenrat, there was another authority in the ghetto that people talked about in whispers and behind closed doors. This is what helped to strengthen the legend that "someone" was watching over everything.

There was only one marketplace in the ghetto — a small one on Krim Street. People would usually start "doing business" there after the workers returned to the ghetto, since many of them were able to smuggle in various items of food. There were instances where "good Germans" among the guards would even buy things themselves, paying for them with food. Often Gattenbach and his wolfhound would pogromize this little market, grinding the "merchandise" into the dirt and beating the poor tradeswomen unmercifully. Some of the Jewish police began following his example, demanding "protection money."

With the help of Zyamke Okun, our "man in the Jewish police," we made a list of all those gangsters and we sent each one a typed letter warning them that if they didn't stop robbing and terrorizing the Jews, the law of the Resistance would be applied to them as collaborators with the Nazis. The letter, which ended with the slogan, "Death to the German Occupier!" was signed by "The Committee of the Ghetto."

The effect was immediate. The trading would go on at the market until Gattenbach or Richter appeared. The Jewish police kept their distance.

After this — and after the "news from the front" bulletins were posted — our underground organization gradually became recognized as a power in the ghetto to be reckoned with. It was acknowledged also by the medical personnel in the ghetto. By order of the German civil authority the Judenrat was supposed to submit regular reports on the incidence of sickness and disease in the ghetto. If the Judenrat had reported this information accurately to the ghetto Commandant, the Germans would have liquidated the hospital and sent all the patients, along with their doctors, to Trostynietz. After conferring with Dr. Leyb Kulik, the Director of the hospital, we sent a letter to every doctor, signed by "The Committee," requesting that the medical charts of all typhus patients read "grippe" or "nutritional edema" or "stomach ulcer" or similar "innocent" ailments. There must be no mention of a typhus epidemic. All the doctors obeyed our order. We met some of them later in the partisan detachments and they told us that this letter had had the same importance for them as a notice mobilizing them into the army at the front.

The ghetto did not realize that "The Committee" had had anything to do with partially blocking the German plan to divide the ghetto area in two. We ourselves even helped spread the version that this had been done by certain "higher ups" who had been paid off. We then made the decision that our underground workshop in Getzl Oppenheim's apartment (which produced "racially pure" documents for trusted individuals outside the ghetto or who worked in the general resistance movement) should begin the large-scale copying of passes for German work-places. These passes were then distributed as coming from those same "higher-ups." We even instructed our people to take payment for these passes, whenever possible, in the form of food products, and in this way we were able to help many hungry families who were part of our underground.

For the first time, the Jews in the ghetto were able to catch their breath — but with that came the revived illusion that maybe the Germans would now let them alone. We then proposed to all our people in the underground that they work to combat these moods of temporary peace and false security. For a long time after Notke Wainhoyz was captured, we could not produce our own news bulletins, until we coopted Motye Pruslin, a veteran political leader, who had escaped from the town of Usda. (His sister Hasye was active in our organization. She and Moyshe Gebelev, who both had a "good Aryan look," organized resistance groups on the "Russian side.")

Most of the time, when we were discussing organizational or propaganda matters, Motye didn't say a word, as if he weren't even there, as if these things didn't concern him at all. On his pale, elongated face lay the anguish of a man who had seen the members of his murdered family falling into the ditch one after the other. Only he had escaped at the last moment. What Motye was thinking about we didn't learn until later . . .

Abraham Tunik found us a new radio receiver and we turned to our youth groups for help in our educational work. In a "malina" on Flaks Street, Nonke Markevitsh set up the radio; members of his group monitored it day and night. One of them took down the Soviet broadcasts in shorthand. We then edited this material and printed it in a bulletin which, for the first time, we distributed on the Russian side. This bulletin, printed by Misha Tshiptshin in the cellar of #9 Ostrovski Street, was accepted everywhere as coming "from above" — direct from Moscow — and again it was a sign to many Jews that "somebody up there" knew about us and was concerned about our fate. The truth, however, was quite otherwise.

By a special messenger who was in touch with Mushkin I received an

[55]

urgent request from Slavek to "write up" all the details of the liquidation of the Jews in the Minsk ghetto, particularly the November 7th provocation. I did so. Later I learned that the request had come from Moscow. Slavek felt, understandably, that the first thing we should tell them about was the repeated massacres that had taken the lives of tens of thousands of Jews.

The result?

We learned about that later. In a note sent out January 6, 1942 by V.M. Molotov, then People's Commissar of Foreign Affairs, "to all embassies and legations of the countries with which the Soviet Union has diplomatic relations," there is an account of all the barbaric acts of the Hitlerites in many villages. But there is not a single word about the total annihilation of the Jews. Yes, there is this sentence: "In the Soviet republics which they have occupied, the German invaders stop at nothing to degrade the national feelings of the Russians, Ukrainians, Byelorussians, Latvians, Lithuanians, Estonians, Moldavians, as well as of *individuals* of other nationalities who inhabit the U.S.S.R.; whenever they encounter them on their path they tyrannize and terrorize them *in the same way* — Jews, Georgians, Armenians, Uzbeks, Azerbaijanians, Tadzhiks and members of other Soviet peoples . . ." (Emphasis added)

In one other place, the note states that on the day after the Germans entered Lwow "they organized a massacre under the slogan of "Beat the Jews and the Poles'."

This "equalization" of the destruction of entire Jewish communities is reported in a similar manner in a note issued three months later, April 27, 1942: "According to incomplete reports the German invaders, in only three Byelorussian cities, killed more than 28,000 peaceful inhabitants: in Vitebsk, 6000; in Pinsk, 10,000; in Minsk, more than 12,000." (All figures cited are from the official Soviet publication, *Dokumenty Obviniaiut*, Documents Accuse, first ed., 1943, pp. 26, 40, etc.)

Not a single word that it was Jews who were murdered and that from Minsk alone almost 30,000 Jews were deported to their death. Babi Yar? The total destruction of the Vilna Ghetto? Not a single word.

While writing the urgent report, however, we hoped that "the world" would learn from us about Hitler's genocide of the Jews and would respond. Thus it was encouraging when Slavek sent word to us, through Zhenka, that our representative must come to a meeting at a certain time and place and use a certain password.

At this meeting there was a report of contacts — loose as they were — with partisan detachments. The report also spoke of the need to prepare people to go into the forests, of the need to collect weapons and to combat the propaganda of the Byelorussian collaborators. The mystery of these collaborators was that none of the local people knew who they were or how they came to Minsk.

In agreement with our objective, Slavek raised the problem of helping Jews get out of the ghetto. M. Gebelev requested that they work out ways to get Jews with military training into the forests. He reported our own attempts to establish contact with partisans. Volodia Kravtshinska, one of our active members and later commander of a partisan diversionary group, went out toward the immense forests near Niegoreloe (formerly the Polish-Soviet border). But instead of partisans, he found large tank units of the German reserves. A group of our young people headed by Fimka Pressman (who later earned fame as a wrecker of German troop trains) set out toward the east. They reached Smolensk — but came back to the ghetto empty-handed.

Zyama Serebrianski informed me that one of the "forest people" had come into the ghetto and gone directly to the President of the Judenrat in complete disregard of security precautions. He told Mushkin bluntly: He had been sent by the Commander of his partisan detachment, Captain Bistrov (pseudonym of a Red Army officer named Sergeyev), to deliver this message. Money and confiscated valuables collected from the ghetto for the Nazis must be turned over to the partisans at once. And what would the Judenrat tell the Germans? The naive messenger from the forest had a simple answer: Mushkin must "show the Germans the receipt that he (the messenger) would give him for everything given to the partisans." (This practice was followed by the partisans when they confiscated provisions that peasants were supposed to turn over to the Germans.) In any case, the messenger assured Mushkin, the blame would not fall on him.

The President of the Judenrat, bewildered by this sudden turn of events, replied that he would have to think about it. When the messenger left, Mushkin immediately reported this conversation to Zyama Serebrianski, who brought me the news. I, too, disregarded all the elementary rules of underground work and asked for an immediate meeting with "the man from the forest."

The meeting took place in Nina Liss's apartment. Before me stood a young fellow of about 18-19. "My name is Fedya," he said as we shook hands. Even a blind man would have recognized Fedya as a creature from another planet. His cheeks flaming from the warmth in the room, his sun-bronzed face was a striking contrast to our jaundiced, parchment-colored ghetto countenances. This man from the forest had no time for caution. He was in a hurry — he had left his horse and wagon quite a distance from the

[57]

ghetto. He spoke so loudly that Nina's mother kept reminding him to lower his voice. I told him to inform Captain Bistrov who we were and that we were ready to help his partisans, but that defiance of the German demands for tribute would only result in new victims of their savagery. I proposed that we send our people into the forest to participate directly in the armed struggle.

I then reported this latest development to the leadership of our underground. After a discussion about this new situation, we amended our basic position. Our new slogan was:

Rateven un kemfn. Rescuing *and* fighting.

The New "Ghetto Passport"

Zyama Okun, our "ghetto policeman," was given the task of assigning only "reliable" people for duty in the neighborhood of the Jewish cemetery. He instructed them to notify him as soon as any Germans or "Black police" showed up there. Zyama knew what a big responsibility we had taken upon ourselves this time. Failure would be disastrous.

He put on two coats with yellow patches, front and back, and waited at the concealed opening in the wire fence.

At the appointed time, Zhenke and another person appeared. Zyama took off one of his coats and put it on the slender young man who was following Zhenke.

Slavek-Pobiedit had come into the ghetto.

Inside the hospital, in Dr. Kulik's office, Misha Gebelev, Motye Pruslin and I were waiting. We all wore white coats. When Slavek entered we put a similar "disguise" on him.

We greeted each other like old friends. Although our first meeting had taken place only a few weeks earlier, the expression in his hazel eyes was noticeably different. They were now full of determination, even obstinacy. It was particularly evident when he spoke about matters that we had to decide together. This was no longer the astonished Slavek of our first meeting whose learning about the ghetto underground was a revelation and who had serious doubts about the legitimacy of taking one's own initiative. Now we were hearing the words of a young man whose personal responsibility for the newly created centralized resistance movement in Minsk and whose experience as leader of that movement had speeded up the process of his political and social growth almost overnight.

He told us first about the general situation, about the widening scope of the propaganda work, and about their first "loose" contacts with partisan units. For us he had special news: the Committee had found living-quarters on the Russian side where the leaders of the ghetto underground could hide out in case of danger. We thanked him for this but explained that we, the leadership, were not planning to disappear in the event of danger; were were more concerned about staying inside the ghetto and helping people to get out. Our request to the Russian side was that they prepare places for Jewish children, as well as for Jewish women with "Aryan" documents.

We told him about the messenger from Captain Bistrov. Slavek's response to that was that we should help the newly forming partisan detachments in a centralized way, that is, through the city committee. As for sending out groups from the ghetto to join the partisans, that depended primarily on the weapons that our people brought with them. Without weapons it was extremely difficult for anyone to survive during the early stages of the partisan movement. For Jews it would be impossible.

To carry out these tasks, it became necessary to broaden the organizational structure of the ghetto underground, which by now numbered some 300 people, plus the youth groups. The "tens" system, which rested on personal acquaintance and recommendation by the leaders, was working well in the ghetto itself, but not as efficiently at the work-places outside where there were thousands of Jewish workers. Slavek promised to help our members make contact with people of the Minsk underground in the work-places; as "Aryans" they could move around more freely.

The decision of the center that we take over direct contact with the Judenrat people gave rise to a difference of opinion among us. The experience up to that point — the city committee itself had established a connection with several Judenrat members and had received help from them — threatened to expose the whole underground operation. (The messenger to the Judenrat from the city committee was a Byelorussian, a former prosecutor.) It was a matter of helping the trusted members of the Judenrat orient themselves to the general situation and having them receive on-the-spot directions from the ghetto underground. (In several Soviet publications there is a photocopy of a receipt signed by "Pobiedit" for various medicines and other items for the partisans. Nowhere, however, is there any indication that all this came from the ghetto.)

Slavek was not in agreement with our policy of looking upon the Judenrat as a collaborator institution for carrying out German decrees against the Jews. Unlike the city *uprava*,* he said, which really *was* a collaborator institution, (even though people from the underground worked there too), the Judenrat had been *forced* upon the ghetto by the Germans. The fact that

---

* Working in the *uprava* was Boleslaw Bierut, later President of the People's Democracy of Poland. He was a speaker on city administrative affairs. He had no contact with the combat organization. The contact with him was through "other parties," who, in 1943, helped to send Bierut to Poland, where he became Chairman of the underground "National Parliament" and a member of the Central Committee of the Polish Workers Party.

almost all the Judenrat members were answerable to the underground was highly significant.

My fear was, however, that this connection with Judenrat people might lead to our exposure, because there were certain problematic individuals in those circles. This argument did not persuade Slavek, however. Misha Gebelev agreed with Slavek. Motye Pruslin said nothing until the very end of the discussion, when he reaffirmed the position he had taken after his escape from Usde. Gebelev, who had been skeptical from the beginning that we could accomplish anything, had changed his mind after the meeting with the leaders of the general Minsk underground. But Motye Pruslin stuck to his original opinion: we must arm our people in every part of the ghetto and meet the Nazis with fire-power whenever they came to round up Jews. He cited the example of the town from which he had escaped. One man had turned on his murderers when the Jews were already lined up at the ditches. This single act of resistance gave the others a chance to run away. Motye believed that our entire organization must become an armed self-defense. We did not agree with this strategy. Our concern was to help keep people alive, so that they could fight and take revenge on the enemy.

Slavek listened patiently to our "debate" and it was then that we learned from him about the terrible thing that had happened in Minsk itself.

Jews returning from their work had reported to us that all along Sovetske and Pushkinske — two main streets in Minsk — they had seen a great many bodies of men who had apparently been shot. From the clothes they were wearing it was evident that these were Soviet soldiers who had been taken prisoner by the Germans. The next day we learned that the bodies were still lying there. For several days there was no indicaton that any of them were being picked up. It was the Nazis' way of showing the people of Minsk what would happen to them if they dared to offer resistance.

We learned also that more than 10,000 prisoners had been marched under German guard to the western end of Minsk. These were all young men, trained soldiers, and the German guards were comparatively few in number. At the slightest suspicious movement of the prisoners, the guards fired their rifles. Most of the men were Russians, Ukrainians, Byelorussians — people who would have had a chance to escape if they had made a break for it into the side streets. No doubt some of them would have been killed by the guards. But no one ran. Not one of them attacked the murderers — as the Jew from Usde had done — in order to create a disturbance that might have given others an opportunity to escape.

From Slavek's story we learned that these men were not even ordinary war prisoners. They had been preparing to stage a revolt against their cap-

[61]

tors. Slavek knew this because he and other members of the underground leadership had been helping in the preparations for the revolt. The leaders of the revolt had been gathering weapons. In the courtyard of the Minsk Poly-technical Institute they had found a cache of Soviet weapons hidden in the stables — rifles, machine-guns, grenades, bullets. In total secrecy they began transporting the weapons into the prison camps through underground sewers. They also made contact with several partisan units who promised immediate help to the uprising.

Among the leaders of the uprising, however, was one Boris Rudsianko, who fell into the hands of the Gestapo and revealed the plan, the prepara-tions and the date it was to begin.

(A report by the Commander of the Security Forces of the 707th German infantry division states that the leadership of the planned revolt consisted of 15 men. The advance unit consisted of 300 men. About 400 rifles, a large number of machine-guns, hand-grenades and other weapons were found hidden in the heating ducts. The number of men ready to join the revolt was about 2500. The expectation was that once the uprising had begun, the pris-oners in nearby camps would join it.)

Slavek told us that the city committee had drawn certain conclusions from this aborted uprising. The main lesson was that all their attention should now be devoted to forming as many partisan units as possible, not based in the ruins of Minsk but in the forests and swamps outside the city. Slavek recom-mended that we give this decision serious consideration. We took this as an answer to Motye Pruslin's repeated demand that we plan armed resistance to the Nazi raids in the ghetto.

Although we partially amended Slavek's conclusion — and the city organization accepted the amendment gladly — the decision of their meet-ing did serve as a direction for our own expanded activity. (This was the only meeting held during the ghetto years with a leader of the Minsk committee.) Our basic slogan — "Ghetto means death! Out of the ghetto!" — was now given a specific direction: "Into the forests! For armed struggle against the Hitlerite murderers!" This summons to sacred vengeance for the murder of tens of thousands of Jews must get into every house.

To help us make certain that this call did not remain an empty slogan, the messenger from the forest made another visit just in time. Fedya came with an answer from Captain Bristov, the partisan Commander. This time he went straight to Nina Liss's apartment. Her old mother was overjoyed to see him — as if he were her own son, she said. She kept repeating that this is how the young men looked when they went to fight the pogromchiks during the civil war. Leaning on her cane, she walked with him to the hospital, led him past Lisa Riss, the guard at the gate, and down the cellar to the boiler-room. (After the war, when I met him with his chest covered with war medals, he told me that his family name was Shedletski.)

Fedya brought us the news that their detachment was ready to accept people from the ghetto, providing they brought their own weapons. Also, they must bring medicines, salt and — a typewriter. In a word, anything useful. Fedya gave us a vivid description of how difficult it had been for the partisan units that had been formed early in 1942. Consisting mostly of soldiers who had remained in the hinterland, or who had escaped from prison camps, Bistrov's unit still had no base, but had to move from place to place after each diversionary action — burning bridges, destroying telephone lines, attacking the "Black police." The village population at first received their nocturnal visits with fear and suspicion, even while they were sharing their meager bread with them and listening to their warnings not to feed the Germans.

Fedya was not too happy to hear that in the future our help to the partisans would go through the central resistance organization.

We began making preparations to send out with Fedya the first organized group from the ghetto to the forest. Responsibility for this was given to Boris Haimovitsh. He immediately got in touch with two of his old friends from his army days, Ivan Kudriakov and Vladimir Dulkov, who knew a place on Kalvaria Street where weapons had been buried. Boris introduced us to the group he would be leading into the forest: Shia Shnitman, Ginsberg, Rilkin, Abrasha Ruditzer, and ten other men with military training. We came to an understanding with Boris that he would maintain regular contact with us and that he would continue his efforts to bring more and more Jews into the ranks of the partisans.

The "exodus" of our first group of fighters took place in a way that violated all the elementary rules of secrecy. In typical partisan fashion they confiscated two wagons in the ghetto itself. Then they built false bottoms in both wagons, "liberated" several horses and at four o'clock in the morning rode out of the ghetto. Their passes showed them to be workmen on the way to the forest to chop down trees for fuel. At Kalvaria, where Kudriakov was waiting, they dug up 13 rifles and 4000 bullets. Into the same hole they threw all their yellow patches and then rode through the heart of the city toward the Bobrowitsh forest about thirty kilometers from Minsk.

Boris kept his word. As soon as the group arrived at the forest he sent one of them — with an "Aryan" passport and a "good" face — back to the ghetto to fetch more people. In the second group — about twenty men, headed by Lt. Leonid Okun — there were also several trained soldiers, such as Jacob

Peskin, who had fought in the civil war, Senye Avrukin, Jaschke and Noam Ruditzer, and others. Leading this group into the forest was Fedya.

Captain Bistrov was especially happy to see Grisha Gordon. He had asked that we send a doctor but, maddeningly, we could not locate Dr. Sibtziger, who had agreed to go. (At a later time we did send him to a partisan detachment in the Naliboker Marsh.) At the last moment we therefore sent Grisha Gordon, a medical student, who became a highly capable partisan.

The third group to go out displayed even more daring than the first two — they drove a truck almost to Bistrov's encampment.

On Slavek's initiative, some of our people joined a group from the Russian side that was going into the forest. And for the first time, we sent out several women of our underground — Anye Bronstein, Dina Beynisman, Sonya Berman, Hannah Rubinshtik and Nadye Ruditzer.

With pride we received the news that Captain Bistrov and Commissar Nikolai Pokrovski had agreed to Boris Haimovitsh's proposal of creating a special machine-gun unit of people from the ghetto. This was the first machine-gun unit in one of the most famous partisan detachments in Byelorussia, and it was the first Jewish partisan unit from the Minsk ghetto to register noteworthy feats of battle.

We now faced a new and difficult task: to observe the secrecy so necessary for underground work and at the same time to inform all our cells — and through them an even wider periphery — of our expanded program of "Rescuing and Fighting." We also had to make clear the methods for bringing this program to life. To begin with, we met separately with each cell leader. The conversations were brief and were held in an almost military, laconic style.

I met with Nochem Feldman, Lena Meiselis, Nadye Shuster and Abraham Shliachtovitsh, a veteran labor leader from Poland. Misha Gebelev met wih Zyama Okun, Mirkin, Lyova Gurevitsh and Misha Kagan. Motye Pruslin met with Rosa Lipski, Hanan Gusinov, Nochem Brustin and Joel Rolbin. With the youth leaders we met separately. Emma Radova, our chief "liaison person," took care of arranging all these meetings, finding places to meet and waiting every day for the workers to return to the ghetto, so she could get up-to-the-minute information from them.

But with each additional contact we made, the risk of exposure multiplied. It was not with a light heart, therefore, that we carried out our decision to meet directly with the Judenrat people. The talks with them had to be under extreme security. They themselves, however, were not too careful about this. In my cellar "residence," during a supposed inspection of all departments of the hospital, I got my first look at the President of the Judenrat.

Ilya Mushkin was a pleasant, likable man with a sensitive face and a high forehead. With the hint of a smile, he asked me how the work was going as he "inspected" the big boiler. Then, as though talking to himself, he said: "I must leave now — get me out of here — I can't do this again."

That same day we appointed Hasye Bindler to be special courier with the sole duty of meeting with the Judenrat leaders — Mushkin, Hirsh Ruditzer and Zyama Serebrianski. Her pseudonym was DIPKUR (Diplomatic Courier). Hasye delivered all our instructions successfully and was given the necessary information on the spot. Through her we demanded half of all the money and of all the confiscated clothing they had collected for the Germans. This we used for our people who were going out to join the partisans. From workshops under the supervision of the Judenrat we expected a substantial part of their production. The soup kitchen agreed to feed people who, for security reasons, could not work anywhere for the Germans. Their duties consisted, for example, of finding and concealing radios, getting exact figures on the available weapons, their location, and keeping them ready for use. For obvious reasons, all the weapons were never stored in any one place.

Inside the ghetto the message of our cells traveled from house to house like a slogan: "Provide yourself with the 'new passport' — a pistol, a grenade, a rifle-part, an automatic — any kind of weapon or part of a weapon. This will give you entry into the partisan forests." Captain Bistrov's condition that he would accept only people who came armed created a "season" in which the ghetto population was busy trying to obtain weapons by one means or another. Primarily it was our underground groups that stimulated this activity.

With the help of our friends in the Labor Exchange, Mirkin, a leader of one of our cells, managed to get his people into a German plant from which they took rifle bullets every day. Kagan's cell armed itself with pistols. Noam Brustin's cell gathered a supply of 15 grenades. (In this they had the help of Joseph Mindel, a journalist with friends on the Russian side.) Feldman's group had been buying weapons all along, even from Germans. The members of Rolbin's cell had the good fortune to find six rifles and several hundred bullets buried in the ground. Their courier, Lila Kopelovitsh, was also able to obtain various weapons from friends in the Russian zone.

Our young people took great risks in this enterprise. Valik Zhitelseif, 16 years old, dug up outside the ghetto 30 rifles and a cache of bullets. Sonya

Kaplinski, Shloymke Greenhoyz and Jaschke Lapidus, with the help of their former schoolmates Vitke Rudovich and Kolka Pryshtsheptshik, dug up 540 bullets near the Mohilev highway, along with a machine-gun clip, 12 rifle bolts, two grenades and other gun parts. The first brand-new automatic — every partisan's dream — was brought into the ghetto by my former prison-cellmate Abe Gelman. From the German arms factory, Celia Botvinik smuggled out all the parts of a Czech Skoda rifle and a large supply of bullets. A group of our locksmiths cleaned and assembled the gun parts. From Emma Rudova we were amazed to learn that Leybl Safran and Shia (last name unknown), two young workers, had taken apart a machine-gun in their work place and smuggled the parts into the ghetto.

Next on the list of necessities for the forest were medicines. Doctors Kulik, Minkin, Sibtziger, Alperovitch, Kerson, Lipschitz, Bliacher, Fanya Safir, Ida Halperin, Bela Kondratovskaya, and the nurses Celia Klebanov and Chinyuk, the pharmacist Chayutin, and others, "put aside" for us bandages, iodine, and other first-aid remedies. In addition, each cell took care of its own medicinal reserve, primarily by "liberating" it from their work places. Thus, Abraham Shliachtovitsh ("Yellow Moyshe" they called him in Warsaw) established contact with a Pole who had been seized by the Germans for forced labor and who became friendly with Polish Jews in Minsk. He soon caught on to why Abraham needed the drugs and he confiscated many valuable remedies from the German supplies. Our active member Tsasia Madeisker set up a central "medicine exchange" for the groups that went out to the forest.

In addition to the warm clothing, shoes, shawls, gloves, and so one, that our people took out of the ghetto workshops, we supplied the partisans with camouflage capes that were made out of white sheets by groups of our women. Also, from the soap-manufacturing shops, a good portion of the production ended up in the supplies for the partisans.

In the ghetto conditions, where the gravediggers could barely keep up with the bodies felled by typhus and starvation, we also helped in the collection of contributions to charity, an activity that was the domain of the wives of our skilled craftsmen. Through them we received the names of people who were still "doing a big business." From this list of givers — by means of a letter signed by the mysterious "Committee" — we requested that they share their food with the hungry. Those of our members who worked at "better locations" set up a "Food Fund" to help mainly individuals who had to keep out of sight of the Germans.

Our work and our influence continued to spread, but our leaders were being spread thinner and thinner. We could not ignore the persistent demands of our activists that we send them into the forest.

However, the chief reason for the decline in our numbers was that as the scope of our work broadened, it became easier for the enemy to find our trail. The Gestapo had its informers in the ghetto too. And many of our own people did not take seriously enough our cautions about observing the basic rules of clandestine activity. Some of them even deemed it a cowardly way to live. . .

Anti-Semitism from Our "Friends"

One day Misha Gebelev brought us the news that, parallel with the Minsk center, some high Soviet army officers who had stayed in the hinterland had organized an independent "Military Council." My reaction to this piece of information was so violent that Misha was shocked. I insisted that he report my categorical opposition to this "tactic" as soon as possible. Slavek, who trusted my long experience in the Polish underground, would at least listen to my opinion.

My opposition was based on two factors. The appearance of a parallel, purely military organization with "credentials" to take over the leadership of the partisan movement — which meant all forms of armed struggle against the occupying power — would reduce the city committee to a propaganda organ. In the conditions of occupation, where the main objective of the city center — led by tested local cadres — was to organize resistance to the enemy by every possible means, it was impossible to separate military tasks from political ones without leaving that center ineffectual and superfluous. My urgent advice was, therefore, that the "Military Council" be dissolved and its leaders coopted into the all-Minsk combat center.

As Misha later told us, Slavek listened to my arguments with an expression akin to despair. He said nothing, except to repeat several times, "Impossible . . . nothing can be done about that now . . ." Slavek apparently knew a lot more about the workings of the Military Council than he was telling us. He knew, for example, that the leaders of the Council — Byelov and Rogov — ran their so-called secret "headquarters" exactly as they had done in Soviet times — they set up a schedule of "tours of duty" and recorded in a notebook the exact time each person arrived, as well as matters that were discussed.

Although we in the ghetto never met with the Military Council, we did — at Slavek's request — express our opinion about some of their decisions. For example, the Council decided to blow up the hall where the Byelorussian collaborationist youth organization would be meeting. (This organization was similar in structure and program to the "Hitler Jugend" (Hitler Youth).)

[68]

I told Slavek that we did not wage war against children, even the enemy's. I proposed that, instead, they blow up only the stage, where the adult leaders would be sitting. The Council accepted my proposal.

Another example. One of them objected to the use of poison against the Nazis. It was apparently one of the more "learned" officers — he cited the Geneva accords. We invited him to come into the ghetto and see how the Nazis were poisoning thousands of Jews in the gassing vans, even though Germany had signed an international agreement not to use chemical warfare.

There was sharp disagreement beween us when the Military Council decided not to accept any more Jews from the ghetto into the partisan forests. Their "reasoning" was that priority must be given to trained officers and soldiers, who were waiting their turn in large numbers. The Military Council also believed that Jews, on account of their physical appearance, would soon attract the attention of the Germans and that this could lead to defeat of partisan missions.

We considered this decision not only harmful but anti-Jewish. It took no cognizance of the dangerous situation in the ghetto, with its daily, even hourly, threat of destruction, whereas the people on the "Russian side" still had opportunities to "wait it out" or to take their own initiative in forming new partisan units. The result of this anti-Semitic position taken by the Military Council was that we had no relationship with the Council at all, even indirectly, nor did we wish to have one. It also forced us to take military steps completely on our own, except that we kept Slavek informed of everything we were doing. And he often met us halfway.

At the same time, we received substantial help from Byelorussians "on the other side" in rescuing children. And this was true both of individuals who followed the instructions of the general resistance organization and those who acted on their own initiative.

The home of Maria Jasinskaya, a Byelorussian woman, not far from the Gestapo headquarters on Kherson Street, served us many times as a shelter for our leaders. For example, we brought Israel Goland there from the Sheroka concentration camp at a time when he was threatened by the gallows. He had been shot in the leg by the Commandant of the camp during an interrogation. Somehow he managed to escape and hide in the cemetery. Our people carried him to Jasinskaya's home.

Whenever Misha Gebelev was delayed on the Russian side and could not return to the ghetto before the police curfew, he stayed at Maria's. It was there, too, that Clara Zelesnik, our courier, met with all our contacts on the Russian side.

We organized a special women's group of our members — Rivka Norman, Genia Pasternak, Gisha Sukenik, Berta Libo and Slava Gebelev — to stay in constant touch with a similar group of Byelorussian women — Voronova, Maria Ivaneskaya, Tasyana Gerasimenko and Lola Revinskaya (it was she who had come with Slavek to that first meeting in the ghetto). The task of these two groups, working together, was to set up places that could shelter Jewish children either with Byelorussian families or in children's homes. Also working on this were Hasye Pruslin, Lena Ginsberg and Genia Sultan. In a short time these women were able to settle seventy Jewish children from the ghetto in children's homes alone.

Slavek also put us in touch with a friend who worked in the education department of the Minsk city administration. The arrangement we made with him was that whenever lost or homeless children were brought to Room #20 between 9 and 11 in the morning, these would be Jewish children who had to be saved.

In view of the clearly anti-Semitic attitude of the Military Council, the help we got from other Byelorussians was comforting and heartening, especially since we could not take one step outside the ghetto without the assistance of people in the Russian zone.

The Purim Massacre by Eichmann's Kommando

No matter how much we cautioned our people in and outside the ghetto to follow the rules of underground work almost instinctively, and most important, not to talk too much, not to boast about accomplishments that should remain secret — it was of no avail. Signs that there were unsavory characters around the Judenrat who talked to the Gestapo became clearer and clearer. A suspicion was gradually born among us that the leader of the Second District ghetto police, M. Tulski (from Zhitomir), was not to be trusted. He always obeyed our instructions to place our own people on duty when we were meeting with a messenger from the city committee, or whenever "workers" were going into the forest "for wood," but we still did not trust him. Sonya Kurliandski, our courier from the Sheroka concentration camp (she worked as a translator in the office of the camp commandant), reported to us that on the day they brought the Judenrat people and the *Ordnungsdienst* into the camp, prior to the November 7th massacre, the only person who had a friendly chat with Gorodietski was Tulski. When we called this to the attention of Serebrianski, chief of the *Ordnungsdienst*, he did nothing about it. He interpreted it as Tulski's way of "distracting the attention of the Nazis away from the Judenrat people."

Our suspicions grew stronger when Tulski started "finding" me too often. One day he showed up in my boiler-room. I decided to get out of there right away. He also sniffed out Nina Liss's flat, where we often used to hold our meetings. Then he started fawning on me and calling me "Yefimke."

When the Gestapo arrested Ilya Mushkin, we tried to find out why. We suspected that the order must have come "from above." But we could not find out. There were rumors that Mushkin had hidden a German officer who had deserted and then disappeared. Another version was that Mushkin had tried to bribe a prison official to free an "important prisoner." In our circles we thought the arrest must be connected with a betrayal from within.

In place of Mushkin as "Eldest of the Jews" the Germans appointed his translator, Joffe, a "westerner" who had come to Minsk when the Soviet Union moved the *Elektrit* radio factory from Vilna. Joffe had been the director. He was a cultured man who probably knew about the ghetto underground, but we never had any direct contact with him. Our meetings with the other Judenrat people who were members of our organization became more difficult and more infrequent.

Then Hasye Bindler, who had maintained limited contact with the Judenrat, came to us one day with an urgent message: they wanted to meet with us at once. There was no doubt it had something to do with an impending disaster.

At the meeting with Ruditzer and Serebrianski we heard the dread news. The S.D. (Security Service) had demanded from the Judenrat that on the 2nd of March (1942), at ten o'clock in the morning, five thousand Jews must report "for work" and that this number must not include any skilled workers employed outside the ghetto. In order to make sure what was going to happen with these workers, Dolski — a well known actor who could speak German fluently — asked whether old people and children could be included in the five thousand. The answer was cruel and unambiguous: *"Ganz egal"* (It's all the same . . .) Clearly they simply wanted five thousand Jews to murder on March 2nd.

Our people in the Judenrat told us that after receiving the order from the S.D. they had consulted with each other. One idea had been to draw up a list of people who were critically ill, or invalids, or old, and in this way to save the younger people. Our directive was that on no condition must they provide the Germans with any kind of list. We must not help the murderers sentence even one Jew to death.

We proposed to Serebrianski that he immediately assign his most trusted people in the *Ordnungsdienst* to every section of the ghetto to spread the word: *Find a way to save yourself.* We urged that whoever could do so should go to work that morning anywhere outside the ghetto. People who had friends on the Russian side should try to get there on the evening of March 1st. Those who had prepared a good hiding-place should go there immediately and stay there. In the Judenrat workshops they had prepared a "malina" for several hundred people. At the ghetto fence our people had dug an underground passage to the outside. We put it under the control of the people who lived in that neighborhood.

A night of terror fell upon the ghetto. The only people who had an encouraging word to say were the older Jews who knew that the next day, March 2nd, was Purim. They comforted each other — "perhaps another miracle would happen and our enemies would suffer the same fate as Haman . . ."

[72]

We did not know then that the *Sicherheitsdienst* had deliberately chosen Purim for their massacre in order to show the Jews that they had nothing left to hope for, there would be no miracle . . .

At precisely 10 a.m. the *Einsatzkommandos*, assisted by groups of Lithuanian fascists and Byelorussian "Black police," began their pogrom. They invaded the ghetto near the Judenrat building and pounced brutally upon people who were trying to take refuge there. "Where are the five thousand Jews we ordered?" The Commander dispersed the Jewish police, accompanied by squads of his own men, to go out and bring in the victims.

Soon afterward came the crackling of rifles and the explosion of hand grenades. The first victims were people who could not move fast enough — the old, the sick, the infants. Then the Nazis began searching for hiding-places. They would stop outside a place they suspected and the Jewish police would call out that "there was nothing to be afraid of." But no one came out. Then the grenades did their murderous work. The streets of Minsk were red with Jewish blood that day.

Their next "military objective" was the Jewish Children's Home. They forced the frightened youngsters to line up and march. At the head of the line was the Director of the home, a devoted mother to the orphans. Her name was Fleisher. In one arm she carried a sick child. Her other hand clutched the hand of her own young son, walking beside her. Last in line was another self-sacrificing woman, Dr. Tshernin. This pogrom on the children's home in Minsk took place (as we learned later) four months prior to Dr. Janusz Korczak's march to Treblinka with the children of his home in the Warsaw ghetto.

The march of the children was halted at a freshly dug ditch at the lower end of Ratomski Street, not far from the Judenrat building. The air was suspiciously still, but the executioners had already taken up their "positions" around the ditch. In command was the Nazi governor of Byelorussia, Gauleiter Wilhelm Kube. At his side stood a tall S.S. officer in a long leather coat. From the German Jews we later learned that this was Himmler's right-hand man — Adolf Eichmann. At his signal the murderers began throwing the children into the ditch and covering them with sand.

The screams and cries could be heard far into the ghetto. Children stretched out their hands, pleading for their lives. Kommissar Kube walked alongside the ditch, tossing pieces of candy into it. (In his official report, S.S. chief of police Strauch described the scene, calling Kube a "sentimentalist.") From the Jewish police we learned that Eichmann swore angrily when blood splattered his coat. Upon the mound of dying Jewish children

[73]

the Nazis threw the dead bodies of their guardians — Director Fleisher and Doctor Tshernin.

At exactly twelve o'clock noon the executioners sat down to a lunch that had been prepared for them on Jubilee Square. Whiskey was plentiful. After lunch, drunk and inflamed, they rampaged through the ghetto hunting for the rest of the five thousand Jews. When their leaders saw that they were not "reaching their quota," they countermanded the original order excluding skilled workers from their dragnet.

At dusk, groups of Jewish workers returned to the ghetto at Shorno Street, expecting to be readmitted as usual. After waiting for quite a while, they began to sense that something was terribly wrong and became more and more anxious to get back inside to their families. Instead, they heard a harsh command to lie down in the snow. As soon as they did so, the S.S.-men and their helpers began firing at anyone who moved. The snow on Shorno and Obutkova Streets turned red.

Directors of several German workshops tried in vain to intercede for the Jewish workers. The warden of the Minsk prison came running — he had obtained permission to protect the brigade leader, Ber Sarin, the Yiddish poet who was one of our underground members. The gentle poet declared, however, that he would go back only when the other workers did. He died with his group . . .

On that Purim 1942 we lost many of our leading people. They lie with thousands of other Minsk Jews in the ditches along the road to Koydanov. We managed to bury some of our younger members who were shot at the ghetto fence in the Jewish cemetery. At the graves of Dovidke Plotkin and Haya Botvinik, who were shot by the Nazis while trying to break through the barbed wire, we swore an oath: *Nekomeh* — Revenge!

I barely recognized Haim Alesandrovitsh, one of our most active members. I had visited him often in his room near the ghetto border. (It was the same room that the Yiddish poet Zelig Axelrod had lived in before he was shot by a Soviet prison guard two days before the German invasion. His wife, Perele, who was the daughter of I.M. Weissenberg, the Yiddish writer, managed to escape.)

I had warned Alesandrovitsh to get his wife Masha and their young daughter Noimele away from the ghetto immediately. On March 2nd she went out with one of the "labor brigades" — and never returned. Haim demanded that we send him into the forest to fight with the partisans.

We began reorganizing our cells. Escape from the ghetto became the driving force in all our work. The possibilities of doing that, however, were now more limited than ever before. The Military Council had accomplished its

[74]

objective. We got no more help in sending Jews into the forests, although Slavek did everything he could for us.

It did not take us very long to reach our next decision: We would now have to organize partisan bases for Jews with our own forces.

Vengeance, Sacred Vengeance

"It's the anger that seethes,
the vengeance that boils . . ."
Itsik Manger

Even during the early months of our combat organization in the ghetto we were already trying, albeit in a limited way, to infiltrate the enemy's ranks, because the more we knew about his plans for us, the more effective we could be in resisting them.

In two instances we succeeded in inflicting serious damage to the Hitlerites. In Minsk they had organized a special regiment of Soviet war prisoners, mainly Ukrainians, to put down any signs of rebellion or sabotage. This regiment was headed by a colonel who spoke Russian fluently. He boasted that a year before the war began he was already in a responsible position in the Transport Ministry in Moscow. He was an incorrigibly garrulous person, this colonel, especially in his conversations with the regimental physician, a Georgian. His most telling argument in defense of the Gestapo terror was that "we learned this from you — the Soviets set the original example with their huge concentration camps." He also pointed out that the NKVD had arrested some 70,000 high Soviet officers, from majors to marshals, and that a great many of them had been shot. That, he loved to explain, "is why the Soviet army has no experienced commanders in the field and is suffering one defeat after another."

Vital information was supplied to us by our underground members who were employed as craftsmen in the workshops of the regiment, for example, Haim Aleksandrovitsh (carpenter), Hirsh Dobin (shoemaker) and Abraham Gelman (tailor). These men made contact with the Georgian doctor and helped him organize a secret group whose main activity was to make the soldiers in the collaborationist regiment aware that they could escape into the forest. (Later we met many of them in the Nalibovki swamps in various partisan detachments.) As a result, the Germans soon disbanded that regiment.

[76]

In the ghetto there was a sculptor named Braser, who was well known in Byelorussia. We met him frequently at Ber Sarin's home. He and Sarin developed a technique for making large portraits from small passport photographs. Braser's portraiture skills became known among the German officers and he was soon being taken to military installations to do their portraits. He would always come back from there with an assortment of food products that he had received in lieu of fees for his work.

We benefited from more than the food, however. The information that he picked up, particularly about troop transports to the front and (from wounded soldiers) about the morale of the men, enabled us to piece together a picture of the general situation. For example, Braser was taken into the S.S. barracks one day and learned the exact number of men who were being sent into the forest to "wipe out" the partisans and in what direction they were going. He also brought us information about the arrival of Latvian and Lithuanian auxiliary police, which was a signal to us that another deadly raid on the ghetto was being planned.

Eventually, however, the Gestapo learned about Braser's frequent visits to military installations. They "invited" him to do their portraits. For several days they interrogated him. He did not return to the ghetto.

We immediately moved his son Mark to a "malina." Mark managed to bury several of his father's paintings in the ground. That night the Gestapo broke into Braser's apartment, vandalized many things and removed the rest. A report of the *Sicherheitsdienst* (Security Service — S.D.) (Yad Vashem, No. 0-53-3) states: "Emergency arrest of a Jew suspected of espionage. He is a famous painter and graphic artist who had gained entry to all German military units in Minsk by doing portraits of a large number of German officers."

Rosa Lipski, a leader of one of our cells, proposed a very risky plan. A member of her group worked as a specialist in a distillery. He was prepared to poison an entire shipment of whiskey that was going to the eastern front during the winter months. For this purpose he needed two things: an adequate portion of the poison and a way to "disappear" with his wife and young daughter. The poison we obtained from our doctors. The "guarantee" that he and his family would be sent into the forest we obtained from the Minsk center, where there was hesitation at first about the use of poison. The "operation" was a complete success. We never did learn, however, how many Nazi soldiers on the eastern front died from drinking this whiskey. (Before my book, *Avengers of the Ghetto*, was published in Russian, the Soviet censor instructed me to abbreviate the account of this diversionary act as much as possible.)

[77]

The Minsk city committee asked us to find an electrician among the Jewish workers employed in the prison. The job they wanted him to do was to install, on the roof of the S.S. barracks, a red light that could be turned on on a certain predetermined evening. This was done. Soon afterward, the entire population of the ghetto was awakened one night by the sound of bombs exploding in the neighborhood of the barracks. From the sound of the motors everyone recognized that "these were ours," and that they "were taking revenge on the murderers."

For the first time, the ghetto Jews, without fear, watched as the Germans rushed into the ghetto like lunatics, most of them undressed, some only in their underwear. These Nazi warriors now considered the ghetto the safest place to be in — the Soviet aviators would certainly not bomb the ghetto! The Military Council credited the success of this operation to — itself . . .

There was a place in Minsk known as the "Factory Kitchen," where the German officers used to have their lunch. Mieczyslaw Kozak, the Pole with whom I made my way to Minsk early in the war, worked there, and he would often come up to the ghetto fence with a chunk of bread for me. He kept complaining to me that he could not make any contact with the underground. He was afraid that the people there didn't trust him. I reported this to the center. Their response came quickly: the Poles should maintain contact with the ghetto organization. In general, the people "on the other side" were very wary of the Poles.

Kozak enlisted several of our women, who worked in the "Factory Kitchen" peeling potatoes, to help him in his plan. Their task was to put poison in a large kettle of soup that would be served to the German officers at lunch. It happened, however, that the German overseer gave the first spoonful of this soup to his cat . . .

Kozak escaped, joined the partisans and was later killed in action. The Jewish women in the "Kitchen" were tortured to death by the Gestapo.

After the Purim pogrom our diversionary work took on a different character. Jewish workers, after their wives and children were taken from them, were ready to face any consequences so long as they could inflict some damage on the "brown fiends." In the beginning, we in the leadership would do the planning of diversionary acts or be given the tasks by the city center. Now the initiative came from our members, sometimes even from people who were not close to us.

Outside the ghetto there was an overshoe factory where many Jews and war prisoners were employed. The Germans kept demanding more and more production for the front, where they were feeling the rigors of the Russian "General Frost." The proposal came from Levin, one of our members:

Set fire to the factory. (In my previous book, *From the Minsk Ghetto*, I reported erroneously that this attempt failed. Soviet sources, however, have reported that the overshoe factory went up in smoke.)

In the Labor Exchange of the ghetto we had people with whom we were in touch for a long time without any interference. Mira Strongin and Rosa Altman were active there in sending trusted people to work in important military plants. In this way our members Lena Meiselis, Nadya Shuster, Fanya Gurevich, Sonya Toyshova, Fanya Tshiptshin, Esther Krovoshein, Dora Berson, Lena Pevzner, Genya Yudovin, Sarah Yudovin and others were given jobs in the former "Bolshevik" factory that was now under the German War Kommissariat. These people engaged in the systematic damaging of material, especially leather. Parachute parts were a favorite target. They also carried out of the work-place, on their persons, heavy underwear, gloves, woolen socks, etc., all of which were used by our people going out into the forests.

Independently of these women, there was a group of our men in the same factory, led by David Lerner, that succeeded in "moving" several field telephone systems out of the plant. These telephones were in great demand among partisan units. This group also made good use of a certain chemical solution which erodes leather and parachute fabric.

Several diversionary groups were organized by us in the factory known in Soviet times as *Oktyobr*. Included among these were our members Silberstein, Shapiro, Noterman, Luft and "Comrade Velvl" in the shoemakers' group; Misha Gritshanik and N. Sukenik in the tailors' group. Among the painters there was Joseph Tishelman, a veteran labor leader from Warsaw, and his 16-year-old son, who was our courier between the workers' groups. The objective of all these groups was to delay as long as possible the completion of orders for the German military, damage as much raw material and finished goods as possible, and use up more material than necessary in the manufacturing process.

The shoemakers, for instance, would hammer countless tacks into the shoes, making it almost impossible for anyone to wear them for any length of time. The tailors, "by mistake," would sew a left sleeve onto a right arm. Whoever could do it safely, carried boots, gloves, uniforms out of the factory, whatever could be used by the partisans. Sascha, a boiler-tender, was a master at setting off short-circuits or fouling up heating systems. A special group, headed by Haim Grovetz, had the job of collecting weapons — and blowing up the plant. There was also a group from the Russian side in this factory, headed by Nikolai (Nasari Gerasimenko), with whom fate bound me up several months later.

[79]

An extremely important task was carried out by one of our groups that worked in the German military communications center on Mopr Street. Heading this group was Reuben Haibloom, a Jewish worker from Poland. After his only daughter was murdered during the Purim pogrom, he volunteered for the most dangerous sabotage missions. Haibloom was well read in Yiddish literature and could handle German texts expertly. In the course of his work at the communications center he came upon precise German plans for the Baranowich-Minsk-Smolensk and the Vilna-Minsk-Smolensk telephone lines. He was able to give us the essential features of those plans. His group also turned over to us schematics on the placement of land-mines throughout the city of Minsk. Two years later, thanks to these diagrams, which were forwarded to the Soviet general staff, many lives were saved during the liberation of the city. The 12-story government building, which had been completely mined by the Germans, was left unscathed.

Another one of our members worked as a telephone-line repairman in the General Kommissariat. For many months he listened in on conversations there and turned over to us important information which we sent on to the city center.

Occasionally our people in these work-places would make contact with Slovaks, Hollanders and Austrians who had been mobilized by the Nazis. By carefully sounding them out, some of our people were able to talk with them confidentially about the situation in the ghetto and the mass murder of Jews by the Nazis.

After thorough preparation and instructions, the German officer Schultz, an inspector in the aviation kommissariat, went out with a group of 37 Jews, by truck, to a partisan base in the forest.

With the assistance of an engineer from the "Hamburg" ghetto, we put out a leaflet in German that even reached some of the German soldiers.

One winter's day there was a "lightning attack" on the ghetto by a group of Italian soldiers who had been sent to help the Germans on the eastern front. They flirted with the Jewish girls, ripped off their yellow patches and communicated to them (in sign language) that they too hated Hitler and all his breed. With the help of our young people, we took advantage of this unique situation to buy a large quantity of small arms from the Italians.

The Purim pogrom showed us that we did not have too much time left. Sooner or later the Nazis would decide that the time had come to eliminate the ghetto in Minsk. Our best hope lay in our own Jewish partisan bases. The underground organization of the Minsk railroad workers was the only one on the "Russian side" to give us any practical help. Their leader, Kuznetsov, a member of the city center, later became Commissar of the famous partisan brigade, "People's Avenger." Kuznetsov offered to pick up selected groups of Jews at a small railway station near Minsk. The system we worked out was this:

A train approaching the station would slow down and the engineer would wave his hand. This was a signal for our people to climb up onto the coal-tender and the locomotive. Alongside a dense woods, where partisan couriers were waiting, the train would slow down again and our people would jump off. We sent about five hundred Jews into the forest this way in a comparatively short time.

Slavek often came to our assistance by giving us locations where we could establish contact with partisan units. On one occasion a large well-armed group of Jews left the ghetto, headed by Kagan, one of our cell leaders. The man from the partisan detachment *Diadia Vasye*, who was supposed to lead them into the forest, did not arrive in time. They all knew our warning: *Don't come back to the ghetto.* Our couriers informed us of the situation. We informed Slavek. He came himself, at once, and led our people to the partisan base.

To the east of Minsk we sent our leading people — Meir Feldman, Lena Meiselis and Hirsh Dobin — with instructions to set up a base for a partisan detachment of our own. To the west we sent Nochem Feldman, Getzl Oppenheim and Volodya Kravtshenski, with the same task. Unfortunately, Feldman's group arrived at a time when the *Einsatzkommandos* were encircling the partisans in that area. Unable to make contact with the partisans, they returned to the ghetto.

On one of these missions we lost the devoted ghetto fighters Sukenik, Arotsker, Pessin and Hirsh Skobla. On account of an error in following the route, Nehemiah Tobias, ("Boyak"), a labor leader from Lodz, fell into the hands of the German police.

But we never stopped looking for ways to lead more Jews out of the ghetto. Vitya Feldman (Nochem's young son) and Sonya Levin went out into the Starotselski forest, west of Minsk, to try to make contact with the partisans there.

One group of forty armed Jews had been joined by thirty railroad workers, but by nightfall their guide had not appeared. The Russian railroad workers returned to their homes, but what could the Jews do? We had provided them with forged documents that identified them as workers collecting firewood for the ghetto. They spent the night in the woods. The next morning a German overseer accused them of malingering — they were not doing the work they had been sent out to do! Michael Joffe, a former faculty member at the Minsk Polytechnicum, offered to lead them into the unknown.

[81]

We instructed Israel Lapidus, a former Komsomol leader, to organize a group that could prepare the way for a mass exodus from the ghetto. Nochem Feldman — after the first unsuccessful attempt — was instructed to do the same. He led his group in the direction of the Koydanov forests.

There was a group of young people in the ghetto who stemmed from mixed marriages. The Germans had granted them the "privilege" of leading groups of Jews to work sites outside the ghetto. They even wore white armbands to distinguish them from the Jews. The entire group became part of our underground organization. Their leaders were E. Narusovitsh and D. Baron. We provided them all with forged papers and they led Jews out of the ghetto, into the forests to fight the Germans.

We also had under our wing a young Byelorussian who wore a "Black police" uniform, but who actually acted as a guide for our people escaping from the ghetto.

The Judenrat workshops were now working for us more energetically than ever. We were able to provide our people going into the forest with a two-day supply of bread, heavy trousers and warm hats. Young Sima Schwartz set up a workshop in her flat where a group of women knitted two-finger mittens that enabled a fighter to fire a gun in cold weather without removing the glove. Rachel Kublin and Celia Botvinik went from house to house collecting winter underwear. In Ida Alers's room a group of women were sewing such "contraband goods" as camouflage capes, indispensable for partisans under winter conditions. Outside the house a group of children would be "playing," but actually they were standing guard.

The movement to break out of the ghetto was outgrowing all our capabilities of handling it. The trade in weapons, the hubbub in the Judenrat kitchen as groups gathered to go out into the forest, the work of so many women's groups on behalf of the partisans — all this resulted in an extremely tense atmosphere. Sooner or later the enemy was bound to pick up our scent.

And he did.

Gestapo on Our Trail

The first sign that the Gestapo was aware of our ghetto resistance organization came after one of our forest guides failed in her mission.

Sonya did not "look Jewish" at all. After leading one of our groups to a partisan detachment in the forest she returned with the good news that she was ready to go out again and that this time she would take with her a radio, a typewriter, some camouflage capes and a few other items. She had come back into the ghetto with a Russian partisan who would help her carry all these things. Some time later we got word that Sonya had been caught by the Germans.

We immediately instructed our people to stop using any of the addresses that had served as meeting-places with her. One of our members reported that he had met Sonya (after her purported arrest by the Gestapo) and that she had asked for a meeting with us at once, so she could turn over certain very important confidential information. We did not believe him. Instead, we instructed a few carefully chosen people to check out her whereabouts. They learned that Sonya was meeting regularly with a suspicious character from "the Russian side" at the home of one of her relatives.

A member of Sonya's family whom we trusted warned us to be extremely circumspect, that Sonya was now in the hands of the Gestapo and that they were using her to get at the leaders of the ghetto underground.

Sonya led the Gestapo to a "malina" where a group of our people, armed with grenades, had been hiding. When the Gestapo got there they did not find the individuals they were looking for, but they arrested several others who happened to be there. They learned nothing from them about us.

We settled our account with Sonya in short order. It was war-time. . .

For us it was a blunt warning that now, more than ever, caution was a matter of life and death, that we had to maintain our contacts only through couriers, that we had to stop using meeting-places that were in any way questionable.

Shortly after this episode the "Russian side" suffered a terrible blow. The entire "Military Council" — about thirty officers — was captured by the

[83]

Gestapo. The leaders — Rogov, Bielov and Antohin — were telling them everything they knew, including names and addresses. Several emissaries who had the misfortune of coming in from the forest just at that time were also caught. The enemy was getting dangerously close to the heart of the Minsk resistance.

We sent Misha Gebelev to the Russian zone to bring their leading people, including Slavek, into the ghetto if he found that they had no place left to hide. In any event, he was to warn Slavek to stay out of sight, since the Gestapo was undoubtedly keeping close surveillance on all the main streets. We could not shake off the premonition that the enemy was hot on the trail of the resistance leaders there, who were not adhering to the most elementary rules of underground work. Their long years of legality were evident at every step. One example among many:

The "expert forger" in the Minsk center had printed up a passport identifying me as a Karaite. (The German army newspaper published in Minsk had carried an article "proving" that the Karaites are not Jews.) My new name — Alexander Duruntsha — was suggested to me by some people from Vilna who had connections with the Karaites.

The messenger who brought me my new passport insisted that I sign a receipt, in my new name, showing that I had received the document. I stared at him as if he had gone mad.

"Whatever do you need it for? To make it easier for the Gestapo to find out my *real* name?"

The man replied coolly: "I am not about to deceive the Soviet government. . ."

We had arranged with Slavek that they would not keep written minutes of meetings. But apparently they couldn't break themselves of the habit of recording all decisions taken at their meetings. After the war, in a wall of a house that was being rebuilt, workers found the minutes of four meetings of "The Committee." (They are still the most valuable documents concerning the activity of the Minsk resistance center: the minutes of December 15 and 23, 1941 and of January 21 and 28. Among other things, they mention the ghetto organization and the tasks we had undertaken.)

Slavek did not heed our advice. He and Lola Revinskaya, having decided to go into the forest, went to meet Partisan Commander Alexander Makarenko at a pre-arranged address in Minsk. The Gestapo was waiting for them. (Several people from the Russian side whom we had managed to bring into the ghetto eluded the Nazi raids.)

Soviet sources describe the fiendish tortures to which Slavek was subjected. To force him to talk, the Gestapo "interrogators" pierced his tongue with a spear. Even from the German documents themselves it is evident that the Gestapo got nothing out of Mustafa Delikurdegli (Slavek's name on his forged passport.) There can be no doubt that it was the leaders of the Military Council who revealed to the Gestapo that "an illegal group of sixty ghetto Jews finances the Party work, purchases the weapons and strengthens the partisan groups." And that "sixty to eighty Jews have been led out of the ghetto to join the partisans." (Yad Vashem Document 0.53, 3/31/42.) Such figures could only have been given by people with whom we were very careful not to have any direct communication, much less give them any accurate information.

As a result of this disaster for the "Russian side" we lost all contact we had outside the ghetto. We now expected the Gestapo to act, though we still hoped they would be unable to find us, since we had had no direct links with the Military Council. Our hopes were ill-founded. Night after night the roar of speeding autos shook the ghetto. Then came the shouts and the screams, the cries for help and the rattling of machine-guns. Before dawn we already had the details — and the names of the casualties.

It very soon became evident that these nightly raids and massacres were aimed at our organization. On Republika Street the Gestapo broke into Volf Losik's room. Leader of a group of trusted people working in a German military camp in Krasny Urotshishtshe, Volf had succeeded in "buying" various materials, including a few guns, from some of the supervisors. Up until a few hours before the Gestapo raid he had been hiding a quantity of grenades in his room. For security reasons we had instructed him to distribute them among the other people in his group. That night he slept away from home. The Gestapo searched his flat thoroughly but left empty-handed. For good measure, they arrested a number of Jews in the building who had no connection either with Losik or with the underground.

On another awful night the Gestapo raided Nonke Markevitsh's room on Sielona Street and found several hundred bullets and a radio. They led him into the street with his hands tied behind his back. With him were his mother and his ten-year-old brother. Beating him unmercifully all along the way, they dragged the family through the ghetto streets to the Judenrat. The last words that people heard Nonke say were: "My comrades will make you pay for this!"

During the night of March 31, 1942, like everyone else in the neighborhood of Abutkova, Kolektorna and Shorna Streets, I heard the noise of speeding autos and then the firing of automatics and machine-guns. In the morning I left my hiding-place — and walked right into the path of Police Superintendent Richter. Along with several other Jews he led me to

Kolektorna Street No. 18, a very familiar address. In one of those flats lived Nina Liss. On the street in front of the building, in the hallway, on the stairs, in the rooms, lay the dead bodies of men, women and children. I recognized Nina's mother. Nina herself was still holding her child in her arms. Richter ordered us to carry the bodies to the Jewish cemetery.

As I stood there, trying to get control of myself, I felt a tug at my sleeve. It was Hersh Ruditzer, a member of our group in the Judenrat.

"Come away from here, quick!" Pulling me into a side street he quickly gave me the appalling news. The Gestapo had raided the house during the night. They were looking for me. Zyama Serebrianski and Misha Tulski of the Jewish police had been arrested. The Gestapo had given them until twelve noon to turn me in, dead or alive, or else all the Judenrat members would be shot.

I asked Ruditzer to take a message to Dr. Kulik at once: I was seriously ill. It was imperative that he send a stretcher for me and get me into the hospital.

Dr. Kulik was able to do it. He put me in the ward for contagious diseases, which the Germans never entered. Soon afterward Emma Radova came to "visit" me. Later she brought Misha Gebelev and Zyama Okun. By this time they knew more details about the massacre on Kolektorna Street. Our courier, Clara, had been wounded, but managed to escape. At around eleven the previous night someone had knocked on the door of the house, calling out, in Yiddish, "Ninka, open up!" Clara had recognized Tulski's voice. The Gestapo had broken down the door and demanded of Nina: "Where is Stolyarevitsh?" Tulski had added: "Where is Yefim?" Nina knew where I was, but didn't utter a word. She died with the child in her arms. . .

What was to be done now? Zyama told us about the uneasiness in the ghetto. Some people were complaining: "Why must we all die for the sake of one man?" Maybe they were right, Zyama murmured. I said nothing, but Misha burst out with a categorical "No!" We must not submit to the enemy's demand, he argued. The enemy has sentenced us all to death, anyway, let's not make it easier for him. Misha tried to convince us with a historical analogy. But it was Joffe, the wise, cultured chairman of the Judenrat, who saved the situation.

He simply followed the biblical story of the "binding of Joseph." He wrote out a ghetto-pass with the name of Yefim Stolyarevitsh, took it out to the Jewish cemetery, where some of the previous night's victims still lay unburied, and smeared the document with their blood. He then showed the Gestapo the pass that he had "found" on one of the men they had shot. Yefim Stolyarevitsh was no longer among the living. . .

The Gestapo left the ghetto even before their noon deadline.

The nightly pogroms continued, however. There was no longer any question about it: they were aimed at our underground organization. On April 2nd a massacre took place at Number 20 Kolektorna Street, where our cell leader Nochem Brustin lived. He and several of his people were killed just as they were ready to leave the ghetto. Similar pogroms took place on Krim, Tankov, Ratomsk and Obutkova Streets.

The Gestapo then began sending agents into the workshops that employed Jews from the ghetto. They checked the names of people who failed to report for work. If someone was unaccounted for they went to his address during the night and murdered his whole family. We tried to save such families by using forged medical certificates showing that the son or husband had died from grippe or pneumonia. On the basis of such documents the names of those whom we sent out to the forest were removed fom the Judenrat records. This method of outwitting the Gestapo worked for some time.

A new decree of the ghetto commandant was clearly designed to stop the exodus from the ghetto. All the Jews were required to sew a white patch on their clothing in addition to the yellow one. This new patch was to contain the exact address of the wearer. And every patch had to show the official stamp of the Judenrat.

In the frequent searches of living-quarters the police dragnet now began to catch people who, according to the information on their white patches, lived in other neighborhoods. Our people tried to counter this decree by preparing extra patches that contained various addresses.

The Gestapo also waged psychological warfare against the influence of the underground. They drove large open trucks, containing the bodies of people they had shot, through the ghetto streets, their loudspeakers blaring in Russian and Yiddish that this was how the partisans treated Jews. The message was: "Don't believe what the agents of the partisans tell you!" (The same death-laden trucks were also driven through the Russian zone, warning that the "Jewish partisan commissars" were killing Russians and Byelorussians.)

Suddenly a different kind of order came:

Every Sunday morning all the Jews must gather in Jubilee Square. The Jewish police urged people to leave their homes, assuring them that this was only a *"sabranie"* — a meeting. People didn't belive them, but what choice did they have? At these meetings Superintendent Richter would explain the newest "rules and regulations," particularly those concerning individuals who participated in "illegal" visits to the "Aryan side." These speeches were also aimed at discouraging the exodus to the forests. People were dying there of cold and starvation, he warned. The German army would wipe out those bandits to the last man. Here inside the ghetto, however, things were now safe — there would be no more "actions." So long as everyone did their work diligently, "everything would be fine."

After the speeches came a "concert." The orchestra of the "Hamburg" ghetto — among whom were many first-rate musicians — played classical music. Gorelick, a noted Jewish singer who had been featured on the Minsk radio before the war, sung sad folksongs that were in complete accord with the mood of the Jews.

These "appeals" were repeated again and again.

But they did not have the effect the Nazis were counting on.

Hersh Smolar, when he was a partisan commander in the Nalibaki forest after the liquidation of the Minsk Ghetto.

Hersh Smolar ("Yefem"), when he was secretary of the Jewish fighting organization in the Minsk Ghetto.

Michael Gebelev — "Misha" — a member of the fighting organization in the Minsk Ghetto. He was murdered by the Gestapo.

The head of the Minsk old city fighting organization ("Slavek — Pobedit"), Isaac Kozenetz. He was killed by the Gestapo, and posthumously awarded one of the highest Soviet medals, "Hero of the U.S.S.R."

Nahum Feldman — "Naum" — a member of the leadership of the fighting organization in the Minsk Ghetto and a partisan commander after May 1942.

Michael Gebelev

Nahum Feldman

Isaac Kozenetz

General "Witold," the general commander of the national resistance fighters (A.L.) in Poland. Hersh Smolar is to his right.

The building that housed the Minsk Judenrat (Jewish Council).

Jewish partisan commanders from the Minsk Ghetto. Sitting from right to left: Hersh Smolar, Shalom Zorin, Boris Haimovitch. Standing from right to left: Nahum Feldman, Vlichia Kravchinsky and Haim Feygelman.

Hersh Smolar, chairman of the Jewish Partisan Organization, speaking at the National Jewish Partisans meeting in Poland after the war. To his left is the great partisan leader Chaika Grossman. To his right is Salo Fishgrund, General Secretary of the Warsaw "Bund" (the Jewish Socialist Organization).

Hersh Smolar telling the renowned author Ilya Ehrenburg (left) about what happened to the Jews in Minsk and in the surrounding forests after the ghetto's liquidation.

(N.B. Chaika Grossman's memoir, The Underground Army: Fighters of the Bialystok Ghetto, and Ilya Ehrenburg's classic work co-edited with Vasily Grossman on the annihilation of Soviet Jews, The Black Book, were both published in English by Holocaust Library.)

Delegates at the post-war meeting of Jewish partisans. Hersh Smolar is clearly pictured toward the front, left of center.

Liova Tcherniak (left), a surviving Jewish partisan from the "Zorin Mint," reporting to his fellow partisan Hersh Smolar on the trial of the Polish fascist murderer Narkevitch.

Partisan fighters Hersh Smolar and Dr. Dora Halperin visit a street in the Minsk Ghetto after the war.

The monument near the building housing the Minsk Judenrat, at the gravesite of hundreds of Jewish children, many from the orphanage, who were killed with more than 5,000 Jewish men and women on the Jewish holiday of Purim in March, 1942.

Long Days, Long Nights and Ever Shorter Months

> "We pray for the day to pass,
> For the night to go by in peace. . . "
>
> Mordecai Gebirtig, *In the Ghetto*

During the day, Jews in the ghetto had one common wish: that darkness come quicker. The security police and the Shiroka concentration camp squads usually raided the ghetto in the morning hours. The days stretched endlessly; evenings seemed to bring some relief. Workers who had replaced the murdered Jews in the German factories returned to the ghetto with news. Sometimes the news was good. After the defeats suffered by Hitler's armies around Moscow there were more and more rumors that the Soviet armies were scoring victory after victory and were already at Smolensk. Hadn't the Germans been bringing their wounded to Minsk from the area around Bryansk and Smolensk? What we didn't know then was that these German soldiers had been wounded by partisans who kept striking at them from the forests.

In the early evenings people went to the "Small Market" on Krim Street to buy or sell something. A few hours later, just as people were beginning to fall asleep, they would be jolted by the crackling of rifles and machine-guns. From the sound of the firing we would try to judge on what streets the massacres were taking place. If it were somewhere close by people would run to their hiding-places where they would not hear the screams of the victims. At such times they prayed for daylight to come quicker. . .

In the ghetto, both the days and the nights were too long. For the constantly diminishing ghetto population it was the remaining weeks and months that were growing shorter and shorter.

With the approach of a holiday the general uneasiness mounted. The ghetto had come to realize that the Germans staged their bloodthirsty "actions" according to two calendars: the Soviet and the Jewish. Even before the pogroms of Purim 1942, several thousand Jews had been rounded up on "Red Army Day" (February 23rd). On March 8, International Women's Day, a relentless hunt took place through entire neighborhoods. Five thousand more Jews were taken to Tutshinka. On Passover and on the eve of May First, drunken Nazi soldiers threw ten thousand Minsk Jews into the pits of death.

It was difficult to estimate how many people were left in the ghetto in the spring of 1942. We knew only that the streets to the left of Jubilee Square were growing emptier and emptier. Into some of those vacant houses the city administration moved Byelorussian families. The barbed wire fence around the ghetto was being pushed closer and closer toward the Jewish cemetery. Everyone could see that the Nazis were moving the "Jewish Quarter" closer to the freshly dug ditches where they piled the bodies of Jews they had murdered in the ghetto.

With the capture of the Military Council by the Germans, we had no further contact with anyone in the Russian zone. The only news we heard from there was the grisly report that on May 7, 1942, gallows had been erected in public squares, parks and at the intersections of some of the larger streets. Hanging on those gallows were the bodies of many of our friends, including several from the ghetto underground. The Nazis let the bodies hang there for days to discourage further resistance, but the result was just the reverse. The anger of the people was mounting to a blazing fury that demanded vengeance.

In this new situation we had no choice but to find people in the Russian zone who had evaded the Gestapo dragnet and were ready to start all over again, which meant creating a new organization with a new center of leadership. We began with Misha Gebelev, who was always ready to assume responsibility. To work with him we chose several people who knew the city of Minsk inside out: Hasye Pruslin, Clara Zelezniak-Gorelick, Bertha Lebo and Slava Gebelev. All of them had a "good appearance" as well as the requisite "documents." Their mission was to find reliable and trustworthy people on the Russian side. They succeeded.

In that same month of May 1942, when 28 leaders of the Minsk resistance organization were publicly hanged, 14 people met in a flat on Torgova Street, determined to reorganize the depleted ranks of the fighters. Before Gebelev squeezed through the ghetto fence on his way to Torgova Street, we discussed with him what plan he would present to the people at that meeting. Our proposal was:

(1) No separate military organization.

(2) Emphasis must be on actions that would hurt the enemy in any way possible. To do this, the organizational structure would have to be changed. Instead of neighborhood cells, small groups would be set up in the most important factories producing goods for the enemy. Their task would be, by every possible means, to sabotage the production of materials for the German military.

(3) Propaganda. They must set up their own printing shop to put out a newpaper, information bulletins and leaflets.

(4) Establish contact with more and more partisan units, in order to send people out to the forests who are able to fight; priority to be given to those whose lives were in immediate danger from the enemy's death squads.

The meeting adopted all the proposals nad elected a central leadership with I. Kovalov as secretary. (His "underground" names were Nievski and Ivan Gavrilovitsh.)

Because of the new situation in the ghetto the meeting recommended that we ourselves determine both the tasks and the organizational forms of the resistance in the ghetto. They promised to help lead as many of our people as possible into the forest.

Our situation continued to worsen. The Gestapo had set up its own "Jewish Committee" in the ghetto. It was called "The Operative Group" and was supposedly within the framework of the Jewish Police, but in reality this group took over control of the Judenrat, the Labor Exchange and the other ghetto institutions. Heading the "Operative Group" were a few highly unsavory characters whom none of the Minsk people knew. They had come into the city with the refugees from Poland. Jews in the ghetto went out of their way to avoid Rosenblatt, the chief informer; we learned that he had been well known in the Warsaw criminal world as a thief and a pimp. In the Minsk ghetto he took to blackmailing people, robbing them and threatening to turn them over to the Gestapo if they complained.

To head the Labor Exchange the Gestapo appointed a man named Epstein who, together with his assistant, Weinstein, investigated and spied on people suspected of belonging to the Jewish Combat Organization. Both of them had had long experience in this "line of work" — spying on labor leaders in Poland and denouncing them to the authorities. In the Minsk ghetto they constructed a special "jailhouse" where they locked up Jews for the least infraction and, when they were finished with them, turned them over to the Gestapo.

We sentenced Rosenblatt to death, but the bullet only wounded him. After a time he surfaced again, more rabid than ever. The death sentence against Epstein was supposed to be carried out by his "woman" in the ghetto

— a former member of the Komsomol. At the last moment, however, she could not get herself to administer the potion of poison with which our people had supplied her.

From inside the Contagious Diseases ward of the hospital it became more and more difficult for me to keep in touch with our activists. We therefore decided to draw two other tested people into the leadership and divide the ghetto organization into two. In the neighborhood around Obutkova Street, Cesia Madeisker was our representative. Around Ratomsk Street, responsibility was given to Shmuel Kazdan, whom we sent into the Jewish Police. Preparation of groups going into the forest was taken over by G. Rubin and V. Kravtshinska.

But even after we took all these steps, we could still feel the claws of the Gestapo inching closer and closer toward our throats. More of our activists fell victim. Vitya Feldman had come in from the Koydanov forest to lead out a group. His father, Nochem Feldman, had helped set up one of our most important bases. Vitya was "an expert" in finding safe routes — in the forest. In the ghetto, the odds were against him. As soon as he arrived, Rubin arranged to meet with him at his mother's home. The Gestapo immediately surrounded the building. Rubin tried to esape. The Germans cut him down and left his body lying in the street. Vitya, his mother and his brother were shot inside the building.

We then turned to Abrasha Nalibotski to replace Rubin. Abrasha was young, spirited and energetic, but the Gestapo's "Operative Group" was getting to know more and more about where our people were — and when. It was not too long before Abrasha too was caught. This left S. Kazdan to take over the day-to-day leadership of our cells.

A group of twelve young men, headed by Valik Zitelzeyf, had constructed what they called "an underground fortress" where — contrary to our instructions — they kept their weapons, ammunitition and first-aid supplies. They had in their "fortress" four rifles, twelve boxes of bullets, some handgrenades, two radio receivers and some hard-tack, in short, everything they needed for partisan warfare. They were ready to leave the ghetto with Zyama, the courier from Lapidus's detachment.

How the Gestapo got wind of this group we never did find out. To the Gestapo's demand that they surrender, the young fighters replied with their grenades. The unequal battle lasted a long time, but all twelve were killed. Only Zyama survived, with seven bullets in his body. Dr. Kulik smuggled him into the hospital, where I heard from his own lips the story of how Valik's group fought to the death.

Hanan Gusinov, our radio operator, also fell into the hands of the

Gestapo. They did not even bother to force their way into the bunker where the apparatus was hidden. They simply inundated the whole building with grenades. For the second time we lost our only contact with the outside world.

We suffered a particularly destructive blow when Misha Gebelev was caught. It happened during one of his "routine" exits from the ghetto through the barbed wire fence on New Miasnitka Street. As usual, he had changed from his ghetto clothing into an "Aryan" jacket. This time, however, a German sentry noticed him. We later learned that the Germans had taken him for an ordinary smuggler. They knew nothing about his connections with the underground. He had asked for some food to be brought to him by friends on the Russian side. Maria Gorchova and another woman named Voronova, who brought him the food, also escaped suspicion and got word to us.

We collected a huge sum of money to try to ransom him. A group on the Russian side was ready to give him shelter. But something went wrong. We never learned what happened to Misha. It is possible that he was killed during a "cleansing" of the prison, when the Germans made room for new inmates. The security police did find the "Jewish jacket" he had buried near the fence, but they didn't connect it with the prisoner Gebelev. During one of the Sunday "concerts" in the ghetto the Gestapo offered a large reward to anyone providing information about a man named "Rusinov," which was the name on Misha Gebelev's ghetto passport. It had been found at the fence inside the jacket with the yellow patches.

Gebelev's absence was sorely felt not only by us in the ghetto but by the general resistance organization in Minsk. He was one of the few individuals who had been involved in the practical work of the underground from the very first day. Now, in my disguise as a "patient" in the hospital, I could maintain contact with the center only through our couriers, and even these possibilities became more and more limited.

Lisa Riss, our guard at the hospital entrance, informed us that the gate was now under constant surveillance by the Operative Group. We warned Emma Radova, Cesia Madeisker and Shmuel Kazdan to contact me only through nurse Jadsha Shpirer and only in the administrative office of the hospital. But soon even this became too risky. The Operative Group had learned that I had escaped the massacre at Kolektorna 18 on March 31st. They wanted to know from Lisa if Yefim Stolyarevitsh had ever passed through the gate. They ordered her to inform them immediately if she ever saw him around the hospital. They went down into the boiler-room and questioned Haim Feygelman: when was the last time Yefim Stolyarevitsh had worked there.

The situation was becoming much too precarious.

[93]

My friends devised a way to hide me even from the bloodhounds of the Gestapo. In the course of one night the construction worker Moyshe Boykin put up a brick wall parallel to the chimney in the hospital attic. They put me in the space between the two walls, leaving a couple of loose bricks through which I could crawl out in an emergency. Through that same opening they handed me food and brought me the news. At the base of the wall they sprinkled tobacco crumbs that had been sprayed with benzine, which would throw the dogs off the scent. M contact was nurse Shpirer, who brought wet-wash up with her to the attic whenever she came to see me.

My new living-quarters were hardly "livable." Sitting was impossible. I could either stand or lie down on my side. I loosened a shingle on the roof so I could get a breath of fresh air and see what was going on in the steet below. The sudden disappearance of people from the street whenever the Gestapo or its agents arrived became a common sight. My only comfort was the news that from both our partisan bases — Feldman's in the Koydanov area and Lapidus's in the Slutsk area — couriers kept coming to lead groups into the forest. From my "malina" I sent messages to Feldman and Lapidus urging them to continue looking for peasant families that would take in older people and mothers with small children.

Lapidus was successful only in the village of Poretsha, where he found homes for forty Jewish children. I also appealed for an end to the internal strife — a luxury that had no place in the partisan detachments. In Nochem Feldman's base in the Staroselkska Forest they needed a leader with military experience. With Sonya Kurliandski's help, our people managed to smuggle Lt. Semyon Gansenko out of the Shiroka concentration camp in a wagonload of garbage. Our guide, Tanya Lifshitz, was waiting and brought him to the base.

A good organizer and a well trained officer, Semyon, aided by our members in the ghetto, was able to form a combat-ready unit which they named after S. Budyoni, but which was more commonly known as "the Semyonovstses," after the name of its commander.

In this most difficult time, suffering one loss after another inside the ghetto, the possibility of sending groups of Jews to this partisan base helped us immeasurably in keeping our underground organization alive and active.

Our Guides

Most of our forest guides were children who, in the ghetto, had stopped being children. Better than many of the adults in the ghetto they had learned how to avoid encounters with the enemy. They understood very well what was in store for the Jews in the ghetto. They quickly mastered the basic rules of underground work. They very rarely smiled. Some of them already looked like little old men and women. And they learned to handle guns as expertly as the battle-scarred partisans.

Vilik Rubeshin was twelve years old. In the panic of the first days of the war he lost track of his parents. Somehow he managed to survive until Sara Goland, a member of the underground, took him in. (Her husband was one of the men we smuggled out of the Shiroka concentration camp.) Vilik quickly caught on to the significance of the whispered conversations in Sara Goland's home, where couriers from the forest were frequent visitors. Vilik wanted to become one of them.

He successfully led a large number of Jews into the forest, until he felt the ground burning under his feet. At that point, despite his youth he became a full-fledged partisan in a unit of the Frunze brigade, where he was known as one of the best scouts and diversionists in the forest. By the time of his 13th birthday Vilik had already blown up seven Nazi troop trains.

When Nochem Feldman went to join the partisans he took with him three boys — Fimke Pressman (Tshulantchik), Abrasha Kaplan and Zyamke Mittel — who had been orphaned by a German "action." At 15-16 they were proving themselves extremely helpful in the work of the resistance. Fimke, with eleven derailed troop trains to his credit, was appointed commander of all the diversionary groups of the partisan detachment known as "25 Years of B.S.S.R."

In the ghetto a new phrase became a sort of secret password — *Dos Kleynvarg* (The Youngsters). Everyone knew that it was children who were leading the groups to the forest, but only a very few knew their names. Twelve-year-old Bunke Hammer had "memorized" the paths leading to the forest so accurately that every bush along the way seemed to have been placed there for his special benefit. This lad succeeded in leading more than a hundred Jews into the forest without once falling into a Nazi trap.

Dovidke Klonski led twelve groups of 25-30 people from the ghetto to the forest. Fania Gimpel had a "special assignment" — to guide our doctors, who were so urgently needed by the partisans. Simele Fiterson was twelve years old when I met her at the beginning of the effort to recruit people for Lapidus's detachment. I wanted to convince myself that we could place the fate of these organized combat groups into such young hands.

Before me stood a small child with the wrinkled face of an older woman. Her clear but sorrow-filled eyes studied me closely as I spoke. Her response consisted of the same Russian slang word that Zhenka had used: *poryadek* — everything will be taken care of. Her hand came out of her pocket holding a small pistol and, for a moment, a proud smile lit up her solemn little face.

But soon, walled up in my "malina," I heard the harrowing news. Returning to the ghetto after one of her missions, Simele had been followed by one of the "Operatives." That same night the Gestapo broke down her door. Simele managed to get to her hiding-place, but her mother and younger brothers were taken away. She became even more taciturn and single-minded as she continued her work — leading Jews out of the ghetto into the forest.

At one point, the Tshkalov brigade learned of the help that their neighbor — our base in the Koydanov forest — was getting from the ghetto. The chief of the Tshkalov staff asked Nochem Feldman to set up a contact for him in the ghetto with Rosa Lipski. As a result, Rochele Priklad and Rosele Rubinshtik were sent to the ghetto on a special mission: Along with people from the Tshkalov brigade, they were also to bring back paper and type for a print-shop.

Rosa Lipski took the two children into her home. The next step was for Basye Tsherniak and Fania Grinhaud, who worked in a printing plant, to "expropriate" the material. As the group left the ghetto, Aaron Fiterman, whom we had sent into the Jewish Police, got them safely through the danger zone and even managed to whisper into the ear of the girls: "Come back again — a lot of people here are waiting for you."

The Budyoni brigade had a strong feeling of solidarity with the ghetto. Many of its partisans had been in the ghetto themselves. Semyon Gansenko, its commander, had been spirited out of the Shiroka camp by our underground. So it was Commander Gansenko himself who met with our three young guides — Haika, Zyomka and Tolik — before they went to the ghetto and personally "briefed" them: what route to take, how to conduct themselves, what to say to the people they were going to lead out to the partisan base.

In the ghetto hospital there was another nurse who worked closely with the underground. Her name was Celia Klebanova. Celia's "good appearance" made it possible for her to move around more easily outside the ghetto. She became familiar with all the paths and side-roads that were less closely guarded by the Germans. She herself led six groups to the villages near the Budyoni base — Staroje Sielo, Skirmontova, Lisovshtshina and Gaishtsha.

At that time all these groups were organized by our members Rosa Lipski, Nadya Shuser, Sara Goland and Sara Iamber-Levin, under the leadership of Cesia Madeisker and Shmuel Kazdan.

In the loneliness of my walled-in "living-quarters," the news that Emma Radova sent me regularly through nurse Shpirer strengthened my certainty that the people of the underground who had replaced our fallen comrades were handling the difficult situation very well. This knowledge emboldened me to request permission from the head of the resistance center in Minsk to go into the forest myself. I did not have to wait long for his answer, but it came at a time when it seemed that the ghetto and everything in it was coming to an end.

Through the open shingles in my "malina" I partly saw and partly guessed what was happening in the ghetto below. From the written reports I received I could sense the heightened uneasiness caused by the increasingly brutal activity of the Operative Group. We no longer had any contact with the Judenrat people. In general, we had no real information on which to base an opinion about what was in store for us in the near future. We knew for certain, however, that we had very little time left. My notes to Emma, to Cesia, to Shmuel, were outcries of alarm . . .

The Four-Day Massacre

There were no contacts whatsoever between the Minsk ghetto and the Jews of the Byelorussian cities either in the vicinity of Minsk or further away. News about the small towns nearby came to us from Jews whom the Germans brought to the ghetto. We knew about the annihilation of the Jews in Borisov. We knew that the "Black Police," led by the Byelorussian collaborator Stanislaw Stankevitsh, had taken an active part in the massacre there. We knew that of the large Jewish community in Orsha only a few people had survived, most of them craftsmen needed by the Germans.

Ever since transports of Jews from various European countries had begun arriving at the Minsk railroad station — from Germany and France, from Poland and Czechoslovakia, from Hungary and Greece — we were receiving from our people employed at the station fragmentary reports about the Jews in those countries. We heard about the various methods the Nazis were using not only to terrorize the Jews but to undermine their vigilance by deception. We knew, for example, that this was done by spreading rumors that the transports were going to work-places in the east. In a roundabout way, news reached us about Ponar — the mass grave of the Jews in Vilna.

And that was all we knew. But even that bare minimum of information left no doubt in our minds that we had been sentenced to death. What we didn't know was the date of the execution, except that it could not be far off. Nor did we know that the fate of the Minsk ghetto was sealed at the same time as the fate of the ghetto in Warsaw. Today we know that the massacre in the Minsk ghetto, which continued for four straight days in July 1942, took place only six days after the mass deportation of Jews from the Warsaw ghetto to Treblinka.

(On July 26, 1942, two days before the slaughter in the Minsk ghetto, Heinrich Himmler wrote to Berger, head of the Office of Race and Emigration: "The occupied eastern regions will become Judenrein. The Führer has placed the implementation of this very difficult order on my shoulders." — From the collection of documents prepared by M. Bernstein, A. Eisenbach and A. Rutkovsky, p. 293, Warsaw 1957.)

[98]

On that morning of July 28, 1942, things seemed "normal" in the ghetto. People crowded around the Labor Exchange, waiting for the German brigade leaders to march them to work. Some of our underground members, however, noticed unusual activity on the part of the "Operative Group." They were scrutinizing the workers very closely, as if trying to spot those who didn't belong there. The Epstein-Rosenblatt gang must have known very well what that day was going to bring.

Immediately after the work brigades left, a line of black trucks carrying S.S. men and Security Police roared into the ghetto. Units of local police and Lithuanian fascists marched in after the trucks. They had been assigned to specific streets and neighborhoods in the ghetto. The "advance" units were the Jewish police. Then, with bloodcurdling yells, the drunken pogromchiks began racing wildly through the entire ghetto. The attack was so sudden that many of the Jews, especially women and children and older people, did not have time to get to their "malinas," which by that time had been constructed in practically every apartment. The Nazis herded their victims into the trucks, which then sped toward the ditches that had been dug in advance.

From my "observation post" I watched as the "Black Police" whipped columns of women and children along Tankova Street. The screams of the terror-stricken women and children rose to the heavens and chilled the blood.

In my despair I turned to the whiskey bottle that friends had given me, but it did not deaden the pain and the hopelessness. All that day my contact, Jadsha, did not appear. Suddenly I heard shooting inside the hospital itself. Not until later that evening did I learn that the killers — for the first time — had invaded the hospital. Still avoiding the Contagious Diseases Ward, they went straight to the surgical floor, shot the patients and all the medical personnel.

Was that the end of the carnage? It did not seem so. None of the work brigades had returned to the ghetto, a sign that the killing would continue.

The night was full of terror. Everywhere you could hear the sound of firing from the watchtowers. Tracer bullets flew through the darkness with a kind of wail that only intensified the fear. It was a prologue to the second day of slaughter.

Jadsha brought me the terrible news: Cesia Madeisker, with her child in her arms, had been shot while trying to cross to the Russian side. Waiting for her at the ghetto fence had been Dina, the youngest of these heroic sisters. (She worked in the hospital and had been in contact with the center in Minsk.) Cesia had come to say goodbye. During the attack on the hospital the Nazis had dragged Cesia out of a poorly camouflaged hiding-place and killed her on the spot. She died without knowing that Meir Feldman, her husband, had fallen in a partisan battle.

On the second day the murderers set out to "check" all the ghetto dwellings. The crackling of automatic rifles meant that they had found people in their homes. Wherever the killers suspected a hiding-place they attacked with grenades. The cries of the dying could be heard in every corner of the ghetto.

Another night came. People began crawling out of their bunkers to fetch water and food from secret places. They gathered up the dead. The rockets and gunfire from the watchtowers were not as frightening as they had been before. The guards seemed to be shooting mostly to cover up their own fear of this desolation . . .

On the third day the end came to the only place in the ghetto where Jews had gathered with any hope of safety — the Judenrat building. Housed here were members of the Judenrat and their families and friends. The Jewish Police had also moved their families into the crowded rooms of the Judenrat and the Labor Exchange. There were also a few Jews who had paid the police for the privilege — a buying and selling of "living-space" in full knowledge of the death that was staring everyone in the face.

All of these people were now driven out by the S.S. killers and pushed into the black trucks with blows and curses. Joffe, the Chairman of the Judenrat, and his assistants Blumenshtok and Tsharno, tried to persuade the Germans to exempt the Judenrat members from the decree. The reply of the S.S. was a series of insults from *Scharführer* Ribe, the "murderer with the white eyes," and a volley of bullets that ended the life of the second and last Chairman of the Minsk Judenrat and his co-workers. The only protected ones were the Jews in the "Operative Group" and many of the Jewish Police, who still had certain functions to fulfill in the carefully designed plan of the executioners.

On the fourth day the brownshirted and blackshirted gunmen rushed into the ghetto with trained dogs on leashes. The animals tore through the streets barking ferociously. After them ran the Jewish Police, shouting in Yiddish: "Jews, it's safe to come out now! The danger is over!"

Nobody believed them. Our people in the *Ordnungsdienst* told us, however, that it really did appear as if the "action" were coming to an end, because on the afternoon of the fourth day they were no longer being ordered to "clear out" the hiding-places. Their orders now were to "clean up" the ghetto streets — to collect the corpses and bring them to the Jewish cemetery.

[100]

In the early evening the Jewish workers who had been detained for four days outside the ghetto were brought back. For the time being, the craftsmen had been spared. When people heard the familiar voices of their own husbands and brothers they finally came out of their "malinas." The weeping that they had been stifling burst into a loud keening that could be heard in every street. Many of the workers found none of their family alive. Homes stood empty. Men wept and sobbed openly. Others cursed in impotent rage. The destruction, the bloodstains on the pavements, the desolation and misery — it all cast a pall of despair over everyone. No one had a word of comfort to offer anywhere.

Through my "courier" I sent word to any of the survivors who wanted to meet with me. I also asked to be taken out of my walled cage. My legs were shaky from disuse. I dragged myself to the hospital's contagious disease ward. Little Rita, who had survived in a "malina" near the Hamburg ghetto with her mother (Lisa Riss), came forward to greet me with the news that two people were waiting for me — Emma Radova and a woman from the "Russian zone."

End of the Hamburg Ghetto

During the Purim pogrom in the Minsk ghetto the "Hamburg ghetto" had been spared. Dr. Edgar Frank, the *Juden-Altester*, and Karl Lewinstein, head of the *Ordnungs-Wach*, were ordered by S.S. Inspector Schmidel, to post guards all around their ghetto and not permit anyone to leave the ghetto for any reason; more important, not to permit any Jews from the "Russian ghetto" to enter.

From the Hamburg ghetto they could see and hear what was happening to the Jews of Minsk. In his memoirs, Karl Lewinstein mentions isolated instances of a child being saved or an old woman being taken into the Hamburg ghetto. The Purim pogrom rid the German Jews once and for all of the illusion that they would survive, that their fate would be different.

In desperation, several of them attempted to escape from their ghetto. Three young people — two men and a woman — set out into the unknown, unable to speak the language, unfamiliar with the neighborhood, and unprepared for the bitterly cold weather. When their absence was discovered, Dr. Frank, the "loyal" Judenrat Chairman, immediately reported it to Schmidel, whose response was swift: The Judenrat must turn over to him 300 people as punishment for the three who ran away. After long negotiations, a "compromise" was reached: thirty tubercular patients would be the scapegoats. The justification was that they were going to die soon anyway, because of the cold.

After these victims were shot the three escapees were caught and brought back to the Hamburg ghetto. They had traveled barely thirty kilometers from Minsk. When they were taken out in full view of the entire ghetto to be executed, they were unrecognizable.

There was another case where one of their young men disappeared from his work-place outside the ghetto and tried to get on a train going to Berlin. He was discovered and shot on the spot.

We were unable to establish contact with anyone in the Hamburg ghetto as intrepid as these. Only one young man (his father was a member of the Czech government-in-exile) escaped to the forest with the help of our people in the underground.

The German Jews knew there was a resistance organization in the Minsk ghetto. They could see the fire that our people had set in the wallpaper factory whose entire production went to Germany. Those who worked on the railroad could see the damaged locomotives and trains that were brought in for repair; they heard from the Germans themselves that this "sabotage" was the work of *"bandit-partisaner."* And yet, living in these inhuman conditions, with no way out, their repeated response was: *"Das ist nicht für uns. Das ist für die Ostjuden."* ("This is not for us. This is for the Eastern Jews.")

With each passing day their situation deteriorated. The "expertise" of the Minsk Jews in exchanging valuables for food was an art that the German Jews had not mastered. They were therefore very often caught and shot when they tried it. The people in the Hamburg ghetto were starving. They could not tolerate the weather. In a few weeks, 700 of their people died of hunger and cold.

On February 8th all the Judenrat members were arrested. The charge: attempting to send letters to Germany through a police captain. They were tortured to death.

Scharführer Ribe walked into a "clinic" in the Hamburg ghetto and personally shot all the patients in their beds. There was no way to help the growing number of sick people. Dr. Sapir, a surgeon, performed operations with a kitchen-knife.

On the third day of the massacre in Minsk, a fleet of trucks came into Jubilee Square, but they were not really trucks. They looked more like buses, all polished up, with little white curtains on the windows.

As usual, the Germans had assured the Hamburg Jews that they were being taken out to work, that they would be fed at the work-places. Only forty men — radio technicians — were separated from the others. The Hamburg Jews were all dressed up in whatever clothing they had left. The men politely helped the women into the buses. When everyone was aboard, the doors were hermetically sealed. The buses rolled away smoothly, quietly, without even emitting any smoke. The deadly fumes were inside. . .

When the vehicles arrived at the ditches, the passengers were already dead.

Only one man survived, a physician. He wet a handkerchief with his own urine and held it over his nose and mouth. He survived to bear witness to this mass murder of the German Jews.

After the four-day massacre, the Nazis had no further need of their policy of "atomizing" the imprisoned Jews of Minsk, of dividing them into three ghettos — for specialists, for "non-productive" people and for the Jews from Germany.

[103]

From the "Aryan Side"

I did not personally know Maria Gorokhova (pseudonym "Mayerova"), the Russian woman who came into the ghetto with one of the first work-groups on the eve of the fourth day of the massacre. How she found Emma Radova, I didn't even ask. The hopelessness was so overwhelming that caution was no longer a factor in our behavior. The main thing was, she came to the ghetto with Emma. The city resistance center had directed her to find out exactly what had happened in the ghetto and which members of the underground were still alive, and what they were planning to do.

According to the information that Emma had managed to gather, several of our most active women members had been saved from death by their well constructed hiding-places. Some of our men had returned with the work brigades. But the overall mood was one of utter defeat, of complete indifference, with no orientation on what to do next.

We told Maria that we expected further attacks on the ghetto by the German death-squads. Our task was therefore clear: by any and all means to make it possible for more Jews to escape to the forest. We were going to draw up for the city center a list of our people now working outside the ghetto, so that the resistance groups in the German factories could get in touch with them and transmit information and instructions through them to the survivors inside the ghetto.

(After the war I came upon a letter which General Kommissar Wilhelm Kube had written on July 31, 1942, the last day of the massacre in the Minsk ghetto, to Reichs-Kommissar for Ostland Lohse in Riga. In the letter he said: "A large number of employed Jews will still remain in Riga because they are still needed in the arms industry concentrated there and because they are needed in railroad transportation." Cited in A. Eisenbach's *The Hitlerite Policy of Exterminating the Jews*, in Polish, p. 244.)

The next day Maria came to see me again, this time with a decision from the center: I was to leave the ghetto and place myself under the "jurisdiction" of the central Minsk leadership.

It was not easy for me to leave the ghetto at a moment when the survivors needed a word of encouragement and hope. As I said goodbye, however, Emma Radova did have a word of encouragement — for *me*:

"With you in the central leadership, we'll certainly have a better chance to do something for the survivors."

I made that promise to the three women who would now have to consult together, act together, and do whatever they could for the Jews left in the ghetto. The youngest and most energetic of the three was Emma. It was she who maintained contact with the center and with the people in the work groups. Rosa Lipski, an experienced communal worker and a graduate of Western University, would be the contact person with the partisan couriers whenever they came to the ghetto. She would also be in touch with the groups that were forming to go into the forest. Nadya Shuser — always in control of herself, never showing any signs of nervousness — would be responsible for disseminating the information from the center to the ghetto population.

Walking in front of me with yellow patches on the front and back of her clothing, Maria had stepped into the ranks of a work-brigade being taken to the central part of the city. At a certain point she signaled me with her hands, clasped behind her back, to "slip out" of line. In a side-street near Freedom Square I ripped the yellow patches off my shirt and followed her. When we got to the Square where the General Kommissar's office was located, I grew more and more uneasy and then froze in my tracks — Maria had stopped at a gate that was guarded by an armed German sentry. I quickly recovered myself and moved closer.

In a combination of Russian, German and sign language Maria was trying to convince the sentry that she had brought a master mechanic to repair the steam-boiler in the building!

Finally he allowed us through and Maria led me into her one-and-a-half-room apartment — in the same building with the offices of Hitler's Economic Administrator of Byelorussia, Wilhelm Kube himself.

"Stay here," she told me, "until a decision is made about what you should do next."

The entire time I was in that ground-floor apartment I had to stay hidden from any prying eyes that might happen to pass by the window.

In my lifetime I had had to "live" in a variety of secret places, but that I, a Jew from the ghetto, would one day be a neighbor of that arch-murderer Kube, Hitler's old "party comrade" — that I had never imagined in my wildest dreams.

Hasye Pruslin came to see me. From her I learned that significant changes had taken place in the partisan movement. The central staff in Moscow had sent representatives to some of the larger detachments in the Kopil and Luban forests. Hasye and Maria Baturina were sent by the city center to General Belaski, of the central partisan staff, who had been placed in command of the resistance movement for the entire Minsk region. The situation was just the reverse of what it had been a year earlier, when the city organization had come to the assistance of the rising partisan movement. Now the partisan movement was helping the city organization. From this I gathered that for the ghetto too it would mean greater possibilities. I immediately sent a letter to the center to that effect.

Meanwhile they began to draw me into matters that had no direct relationship to the ghetto. One of my visitors was Vatik (Nikoforov), who had been fortunate enough to escape the trap the Gestapo had set for the first committee. We had met early in 1942 to write a bulletin that was to be printed in our ghetto printing-shop.

The General Kommissariat over Byelorussia had begun setting up a number of collaborationist organizations whose function was to collect winter relief, to organize cultural events, to organize the young people — all of this on the model of the Hitler organizations in Germany itself. Later they created a military institution known as *Samaakhova* — "Byeolorussian National Defense" — to combat the partisan movement. No one in the Minsk center, which had decided to fight these collaborationists, knew the individuals who headed these pro-Hitler groups. There was not even one native of Minsk among them. Most of them came from Vilna and Warsaw. The top man, Fabian Akintshitz, came directly from the staff of Reichs-Minister Rosenberg. I was the only one who knew these characters. Through my political activity in the 1930s I had encountered some of them personally. With others I had polemicized in the press.

I knew that Akintshitz was an official representative of the Rosenberg staff and was the real leader of the Byelorussian collaborationists. In the 1920s he had had something to do with the Byelorussian national liberation movement and served a sentence in the Lukishki prison in Vilna. (The Polish political police had blinded one of his eyes.) In the 1930s "the one-eyed devil" had gone over to the Nazis. His chief deputy was Vladimir Kaslovski, editor of the *Belaruskaia Gazeta*, who filled every issue of his collaborationist sheet with the vilest anti-Semitic attacks.

Heading the so-called "Byelorussian Loyalty Council" (later changed to Byelorussian Central Concil) was the former director of the Byelorussian secondary school in Vilna, Romuald Ostrowski, who had been prominent in the *Sanacja* government in Poland. His aide was the former Deputy of the Polish Sejm, Sovolewski. Others in this clique were Dr. Tumash, mayor of

Minsk, and Vatslav Ivanovski, whose primary occupation was robbing the ghetto population, including the starvation portions of food that had been allocated to the Jews by the German authorities. Stanislaw Stankewicz, the mayor of Borisov, was also part of this collaborationist leadership.

In the late 1920s I had met Sejm Deputy Sobolewski, along with Sakowicz, then a student at Vilna University, who became the Commandant of the Byelorussian police in 1942. In the ghetto it was rumored that Sakowicz would release Jews caught by the police in the Russian zone and that in general he gave the impression of not being a Nazi collaborationist at heart. I had asked our city leadership for permission to meet with Sobolewski, whose son was an officer in the Soviet army, and also with Sakowicz, because I thought I could persuade them to help the resistance movement. My offer was rejected. At the same time they chided me with the reproach that such naivité did not become me. Sakowicz was later killed when his car hit a partisan mine.

By sentence of the resistance center, Akintshitz, Kaslovski and Ivanovski were shot to death.

Hiding in a corner of Maria's room I wrote a detailed report about the nature of the collaborationist organizations and their leaders. (This document was luckier than the report I wrote about the mass murder of the Jews of Minsk, which was squelched by the Ministry of Information. On the basis of my report an article on the Byelorussian collaborators was published in the Moscow *Pravda*.)

During the time I spent in this hiding-place I sent to the ghetto, with the help of Hasye and Maria, a number of reports, trying to encourage the people of the underground with promises of help from the city center. Despite her Jewish appearance, Emma Radova also took the risk of meeting with me. She firmly requested permission to leave the ghetto as soon as possible. She was almost certain that the "Operative Group" had her under surveillance.

Permission for her to go out to the forest was granted, but it came too late. While waiting for the "mail" that workers usually brought back with them into the ghetto, she was detained by Epstein, the head of the "Operatives," who immediately turned her over to the Gestapo. From prison I received a message that Emma had not broken under torture. She had not revealed a single name of her many contacts both in the ghetto and the Russian zone. The only thing she requested was that we get a cyanide tablet to her as quickly as possible. On January 9, 1943 Emma Radova perished in a Gestapo prison.

In August 1942, soon after Emma's arrest, I received permission to leave the ghetto. I asked for a guide to take me toward the western forests, where many of the organizers of the ghetto underground had already joined the partisans.

Inside the Minsk ghetto there was no longer any organization; no cells, no youth groups. Only individuals authorized to receive couriers from the forests and to prepare groups to leave the ghetto remained. Primarily these were Rosa Lipski and Nadya Shuser — both of whom had tried to get out of the ghetto and failed — Sara Goland, Sara Levin and a few others. All of them were given permission to leave the ghetto as soon as they found replacements and addresses where the forest couriers could stay.

After the four-day massacre there were about 12,000 Jews remaining in the ghetto. (German documents give the figure as 8794 — they did not know about the people in the *malinas*, among them many women and children.) It was clear to us that it was now more urgent than ever for the underground to conduct its work from partisan bases. The trouble was that after the massacre we had no more contact with the partisan detachments that had been set up by our people. Now that I was leaving the city, it might be possible again to establish contact and to organize a leadership group at our forest base that would concern itself with the survivors in the ghetto.

A new German word now made its appearance in the ghetto: *Kasernirung*. This meant that the most qualified workers in the ghetto were compelled, after their day's work, to sleep in a barracks. Only on Sundays were they permitted to return to the ghetto. Every morning the surviving Jews had to report at the Labor Exchange where German foremen from the work-sites would come and select the "hands" that they needed, mostly women, for cleaning, washing and kitchen work. Men were taken for heavier work such as cement-mixing and loading trucks. People would come back hungry and dead tired, but they still preferred to be outside the ghetto during the day.

We informed the city combat organization that Jewish craftsmen were being *Kasernirt* in the following factories: Miasnikov, Voroshilov, Oktyober, Bolshevik, Kuybishev, Red Dawn, Belarus, Radio Factory, Main Printing Plant, Meat Combine, Elektro Station, Bread Factory, "Automat," Gasoline Base, and the German enterprises, Borman, Sharov-Werke, Trebetz and Trol.

We proposed that trustworthy people from the Russian side contact our workers in the factories about going out to the forest. This plan was only partially successful. From Work Camp #13 (in Grushevski Posyolok), Jews went out with the city workers to join the partisans.

After each such episode the S.S. and the police would go searching in the ghetto for the Jews who had escaped. It always ended with new victims. . .

The perspective of leading more Jews out of the ghetto seemed to us to be more realistic after I left my "Aryan" hiding-place and went out to the forest base.

But it didn't turn out that way.

Toward the Goal — Without a Guide

In broad daylight Maria led me to the Tchervenski Market, where she had arranged for me to meet my guide to the Koydanov forest. I walked up and down among the "tradesmen" as they kept asking me, in their veiled language, what kind of merchandise I was looking for. Meanwhile, I tried to avoid the eyes of police and other suspicious persons.

But the man I was waiting for did not appear. The hour grew later and later. I had no idea what to do next. I could not go back to Maria's; the German sentry there was sure to stop me. I hid in the corner of a courtyard from which I could observe the marketplace. Soon it would be dark, and still there was no sign of the courier . . .

I made my way to a little woods nearby where I could wait till morning. Fortunately for me, Soviet aircraft were bombarding military objectives in the area. No one else came into the woods.

At daybreak I went to the home of Veremeitshik, a member of the city committee. She had once been a lecturer at the University of Minsk. If she was surprised to see me, she didn't show it. She simply locked me up in her one room and went out to consult with "Nikolai" (Nazari Gerasimenko). He instructed her to bring me to his apartment at 25 Niemega Street early that evening, before the police curfew. No doubt for me to be in the home of one of the leaders of the city center was a violation of security, but at that moment we had no alternative, especially since I was on my way to the forest.

At Nikolai's I met with several other leaders of the underground. Niewski (Kavaliov), who was secretary of the committee, told me that they had a carefully worked out plan to send about 5000 men out to the twenty partisan detachments with which the center had direct communication. Included in that number were many Jews from the ghetto. I sent that information to our leadership in the ghetto, urging them to get as many people ready as possible.

My continued presence in Nikolai's apartment, which the Minsk underground used as a meeting-place, was extremely dangerous. We arranged with his wife Tanya that in case of emergency Nikolai and I would step out through the window onto the roof of a shed that led into the cellar. Their eleven-year-old daughter Lusia was always "on duty" at the gate of the building, but it was not always possible to know what was going on, because there was a brothel there that was frequented by German soldiers.

Nikolai came home that evening exhausted from a trip to a partisan base, where he had made arrangements for them to receive people from Minsk. At midnight we were aroused by a hammering at the door. Tanya helped me get out through the window. In my underwear, I stretched out on the tin roof between the windows. Nikolai, who started to put on his clothes, did not get to the window in time. In their customary brutal manner, the Gestapo smashed their way in. One of them rushed over to the window and shone his flashlight, but did not see me. And they paid no attention to the clothing that was piled next to my bed . . .

When I heard the door being closed again I lowered myself to the ground to see whether the Gestapo had posted a guard at the building. No one was there, but I could see the faces of the neighbors pressed against the windows. I climbed back up on the roof and into Nikolai's apartment; it looked like the scene of a pogrom. I dressed quickly and from behind the wallpaper took the documents I had received from the partisan general staff.

I left the building and started back toward the ghetto. Near the fence I ducked into a demolished structure. For two days and nights it served as my shelter and my observation post as I kept looking for a familiar face among the workers returning to the ghetto. On the third day I noticed our old activist Abraham Shliachtovitsh among the group of workers. I slipped in among them and he immediately decorated me with a set of yellow patches.

Famished and exhausted, I arrived at Henyek Zucker's room on Tankova Street. From Shliachtovitsh I had learned that Niemiga Street was blocked off — apparently the Gestapo was looking for me. Later that day notices were posted all over the city offering a reward to "anyone who brings in Yefim Stolyarevitch dead or alive."

Through Shliachtocitsh I proposed to the city committee that a group prepare to go into the forest with me and try to reach the partisans, even without a guide. Four men were ready to leave with me. Two of them were the "westerners" Reuben Haibloom and Nochem Goldsack. They had smuggled out of their workplace a few guns that had been packed up for a Berlin exhibit of captured partisan weapons. The other two were natives of Minsk — David Lungin, who had fought in the civil war, and Grisha Freedman, who had left the ghetto once before but was forced to return.

Henyek Zucker got me "settled" in a ditch in the courtyard that had been

[111]

dug as a hiding-place for materials of various sorts. I breathed through a long pipe that stuck out of the dirt covering the ditch. The candle that I lit went out after a few minutes for lack of oxygen.

Before we left, Rosa Lipski heard disastrous news from Dina Madeisker in the Russian zone. The central resistance organization in the city had completely collapsed. One of the men arrested had revealed everything he knew to the Gestapo. All over the city, people were being picked up. Dina had gone out alone to try to find a partisan unit. Our last link with the Russian side was broken. Whatever we did now would have to be done with our own forces.

We learned later that it was Kavaliov, the secretary of the center, who had been broken in the Gestapo torture chambers. He had even agreed to speak at workers' meetings and confess his "sins." At one such meeting in the Miasnikov factory he had "proven" how futile it was to resist the "mighty, invincible German army." What happened to him afterward is not known.

According to Soviet sources, Nikolai, his wife Tanya and their daughter Lusia were burned alive in Trostinyetz, the "Byelorussian Treblinka."

No other general resistance center was ever created in Minsk. Diversionary groups were organized directly from the forests to fight against the Nazi terror machine and the German army of occupation. One of their most telling blows was the bomb that was placed in the bed of Wilhelm Kube, General Kommissar of Byelorussia and Hitler's "oldest party comrade." This was the daring work of Yelena Mazanik, a "servant-girl" in his house, assisted by a group of partisans.

Sixteen hundred Nazi soldiers were killed in Minsk by the underground in such diversionary acts. They are buried in a German military cemetery.

Early in the morning, at a prearranged time, they dug me out of the ditch and the five of us took our places in a group going out to a brick-works at the western end of the city.

Thus it came about that after having provided thousands of Jews with guides or with detailed maps into the forests, we five set out "to look for the wind in the field," as the Russian saying goes. I remembered which partisan brigades and detachments were based in the Koydanov forest, but exactly where I had no idea. So we proceeded blindly, and on the very first day almost fell into the hands of the S.S.

We walked along field-paths, not main roads, hoping in this way to avoid any "unfriendly" chance encounters. Each of us carried a gun and an ampule of poison. We had agreed amongst ourselves that we would use our weapons — or the poison — only on my command. In a valley where we sat down to rest we gradually became aware of men shouting to each other in German.

[112]

Nochem Goldsack went to reconnoiter and came right back with the alarming news that an S.S. squad was combing the area and heading in our direction. It was too late to make a run for it. We decided to keep out of sight as long as possible, but to fight to the end if the S.S. came too close. We flattened out on the ground, ready to fire our weapons to the last bullet — but saving the last one for ourselves. I put the cyanide tablet in my mouth. Meanwhile, the shouts of the S.S.-men — *"Banditen, raus!"* — were growing louder and louder.

Suddenly there was another kind of yell:

"Mahl zeit!" ("Chow")

We watched as the figures closest to us turned and retreated in the opposite direction . . .

For two weeks we hid in the forest during the daylight hours. Now and then David Lungin, who looked and spoke like one of the local farmers, went into a village to buy food.

While he was at it, he also tried to find out where the Germans were. When he asked about "our brothers in the forest," however, he always got the same answer: *"Nitshoho nie viedayu"* — (I don't know anything).

(Later, from the partisans, we learned that the villagers had been telling the brothers in the forest about "five wanderers" who kept asking how they might meet the "forest people.")

One bright day, as we were resting after our all-night hike, we found ourselves surrounded by a group of armed men.

"Lay down your weapons!"

We had agreed never to surrender our weapons voluntarily to anyone. As we reached for our guns, I told our captors that we were on a special mission, that we were carrying important documents from the central partisan staff. This seemed to convince them. From my conversations with Nikolai I recalled the name Subotin, commander of the Frunze brigade. I asked permission to speak to him. The group led us to the village of Viertniki, fed us, and told us to wait there.

Next morning, according to instructions, the five of us went to the rim of a forest. Suddenly and silently, three men "grew out of the earth" and blocked our way. Each one was dressed differently, but wore a military cap decorated with little stars. Again we went through the same ritual. The stoutest of the three — who turned out to be Subotin himself (Captain Serebriakov) — ordered us to lay down our weapons. I told him that our weapons were for fighting the enemy, not for lying on the ground.

The three men stepped up and shook our hands.

"Excellent!" said Subotin. "You've passed the first test!"

[113]

He already knew about the collapse of the Minsk center. Brigade Commissar Vautshuk read the statement of the central partisan staff regarding the rescue of the civilian population. I described the situation in the ghetto and emphasized the urgency of bringing as many people as possible into the forest. Chief-of-Staff Anokhin took the list of ghetto contacts from me and promised to discuss the matter with his fellow officers. We five were instructed to wait in the village for an answer from the Frunze staff.

After days of anxious wandering and trying to outguess the enemy, we were finally able to relax a little in the village, where we were received in a friendly manner and got a good night's sleep. The villagers themselves took turns standing guard against any Nazi surprise attack during the night.

The next day a middle-aged man in a makeshift uniform arrived and greeted us in a pure Minsk Yiddish:

"*Vos makht it, khevra?*" (How are you, guys?)

I'm afraid we stared at him most impolitely. His features were typically Slavic. He was actually a Byelorussian named Mihail Kashinski, but he had grown up among Yiddish-speaking Jews. Up until the war he had been chief of the military district. He told us that he had been assigned by the Frunze staff to help us organize a new partisan unit and that there were three steps in the process: One, to find a place in the forest for our base. Two, to find a source of food over which we could exercise some control. Three, to send a courier to the ghetto to bring back more people, primarily those who had weapons.

In the evening, Kashinski took me along to a nearby village where he had called a meeting of the young people. I spoke to them about the atrocities the Germans had committed in Minsk. I reported the latest news from the war fronts, as much as I knew of it. Kashinski concluded the meeting with an "announcement" that all the young people, since they had an obligation to serve in the army, were now being mobilized into the ranks of the partisans, and that they would have a brief period in which to prepare for their new life in the forest.

This was the *first and only* instance in my partisan experience where young people were mobilized not as volunteers but as conscripts. The result of that policy turned out to be a tragic one.

Kashinski appointed me Commander of the first mobilized group. Quite accidentally I found a common language with them.

The next day Kashinski came from Frunze staff headquarters accompanied by a blond, typically Byelorussian woman and asked me to "fill her in" about the latest developments in the ghetto and to give her the names of our contacts. I must have stared at her in such surprise that she let me have it in a juicy Minsk Yiddish:

"What's the matter, you don't like the way I look? So don't marry me! But first let's introduce ourselves. My name is Bronye. My mother called me Braindl. By profession I'm a schoolteacher — I worked in a village school until the cutthroats came . . ."

From autumn 1942 to January 1943 Bronye succeeded in bringing so many Jews into the forest that it became necessary to form a new unit.

Thus, thanks to the Jews from the Minsk ghetto, there were now three units, which later combined to become the Frunze partisan brigade.

The Jewish Forest Leadership

The renewed contact with the Minsk ghetto was of great significance — not least for morale — for all those who were waiting anxiously to go into the forest. In place of despair came hope — which was much greater than the situation warranted. With the help of people from the ghetto another partisan unit was formed, with Zaskin as Commander. However, the total number of Jews that Bronye could bring out of the ghetto to our base was still quite limited.

I discussed this problem with several partisans whom we had worked with while we were all in the ghetto — Lt. Aaron Smushkevitch, Hersh Solomonik, Israel Goland, Henyek Zucker, Abraham Shliachtovitsh (he had been appointed "Quartermaster" of our detachment), Jadshe (who immediately had a lot of work to do — two of our men were wounded while learning how to use their weapons), as well as with my "traveling companions" Reuben, Nochem, David and Grisha. We all reached the same conclusion: If we relied only on our two units in the Frunze brigade, the help we could give the ghetto would be merely a drop in the vast sea of Jewish troubles. We had to make contact with other partisan units and ask for assistance.

First I had to find Nochem Feldman, which wasn't easy, and not because of the distance between our units. When I asked my commander for permission to contact the Budyoni brigade, his reply was reproachful: "You haven't even smelled gunpowder yet and already you want to join another unit?" I told him the truth about my concerns. He said nothing, but the next day he assigned someone to go with me and pointed me in the direction of the "Semyonovtses."

When I met Feldman, there was a repetition of the scene that had taken place two years earlier in the ghetto. To my proposal that he and I — who had both been in the leadership of the ghetto resistance movement — should form a similar group in the forest to help the ghetto, his immediate response was that an exclusively Jewish leadership like that would be neither recognized nor permitted. Besides, he argued, it might even play into the hands of the anti-Semitism that had been sharpened by the Nazi propaganda.

[116]

There was a lot of truth in that. Out here in the forest we were totally dependent upon our commanders; we could not act independently, as we had done in the ghetto. Nevertheless, we both finally agreed on the following:

(1) We would meet with the staff of the Budyoni brigade, in which the Jews of Minsk — notably Feldman himself — were playing a big part, and ask for help for the ghetto.

(2) Personally we would urge Jewish partisans to be in the front lines during combat, so as to avenge the Jews who had been tortured and murdered by the Nazis.

(3) We would meet and consult with each other as often as possible about steps to take on behalf of the ghetto. We would not "legalize" these meetings, however, but would work through the general partisan leadership.

That same day we met with the commander of the Budyoni brigade, primarily to consider the documents I had brought with me from the central partisan staff. It was the first time I had met Semyon Gansenko. With him was Verhotzev, his chief of staff. Our comments seemed to impress them. We pointed out that it was the ghetto that was now in the most immediate danger and that we wanted to get the maximum number of Jews out of that trap. And that this applied not only to young, combat ready people but to everyone without exception. Commander Gansenko promised to call his entire staff together immediately to consider what could be done.

Early the next morning the entire Budyoni detachment was lined up and the latest staff decision was read to them: "In accordance with orders from the central partisan staff concerning the rescue of the civilian population, the staff of the Budyoni brigade has decided to create a special base in the forest between the villages of Viertniki and Novosady in the Koydanov region, and to bring as many people as possible there from the Minsk ghetto. Those who are able to fight must be given an opportunity to avenge the blood of their parents, brothers and sisters. The Budyoni brigade has selected five of its partisans, headed by Kasimir Zherobin, to organize and assist this base for the Jews of Minsk. Under their supervision, fifteen rifles have been allocated for newcomers with military training."

Thus began the history of Unit #106, consisting of Jews from Minsk. Appointed commander was Sholem Zorin, a construction worker and former civil war partisan. Later, Anatole Wertheim, who had served in a Polish partisan detachment, was appointed chief of staff. Haim Feygelman, my "foreman" in the hospital boiler-room, was named Commissar of this unit, which the partisans in the region called "Zorintses."

The second objective — to urge the Jewish partisans to be in the front

[117]

lines everywhere, but especially in the diversionary groups — found its greatest response in various units when we moved our base from the Koydanov forest to the Naliboki swamp.

The third objective — to meet and consult with each other frequently about helping the ghetto — became much easier with the formation of Zorin's unit. (We held our meetings among the Minsk "Jews without yellow patches.") Several of our ghetto activists came in with the groups which the "youngsters" and the "Zorintses" guides brought into the forest. In accordance with our instructions, they had prepared other people to take their place — mostly women — and arranged shelter for our couriers from the forest.

At the first meeting, which took place in a far corner of our forest base, the following were present: Commander Zorin, Rosa Lipski, Nadya Shuser, Nochem Feldman and myself. We heard a full report about the situation in the ghetto and planned immediate steps to increase the number of Jews brought into the forest.

Successes, Failure, Defeats

The news from the ghetto that reached us through returning couriers was truly encouraging. The people we had left in leadership were doing everything possible to prepare Jews to get out — instructing them on where to go, what to take with them, and so on. On their own, individuals were also trying to obtain gifts of tobacco, underwear, warm socks, gloves.

Great hopes were raised by Dora Berson's return to the ghetto. She had been sent into the Rudinsk area to re-establish contact with Israel Lapidus's partisans. She had also made contact with the Second Minsk Partisan Brigade and learned that they were ready to accept Jews from the ghetto. She had even managed to obtain a truck and brought a group right to the partisan base. Young and energetic, Dora had come back to the ghetto with an "order" for a radio receiver — the only way we had of keeping in touch with the "outside world." But that was the last trip Dora Berson made to the ghetto. Resisting the police she died a hero's death.

The continuous reports we received about the murderous acts of the S.S. were unbearably painful. The Jewish traitors in the "Operative Group" kept informing the German authorities of individuals "suspected of connections" with the partisans. They reported, for example, that at 45 Obutkova Street there was a young man hiding weapons. All 140 occupants of that building were shot to death.

In the yard of a large garage where captured weapons were stored, the Germans hung our underground worker Hosenpud and three Russian prisoners for smuggling out guns. This did not stop Katya Tsirlin and Celia Botvinik, whom our people in the Labor Exchange had sent to work in that same garage, from continuing their activity. The two young women set up a system whereby they could slip rifle parts to Grisha Sorvanyetz, our eleven-year-old courier. This brave lad would then run the stuff over to Isaac Murokh, a railroad worker who had ways of getting the parts into the ghetto.

Katya and Celia also managed to get permission from the German foreman to take wood-shavings home with them for heating their cold room in the ghetto. Amidst this "kindling," however, were also rifle parts. And inside their big rubber boots they would drop small bullets. All of this was brought out to the forest, where our mechanics assembled the parts into usable weapons.

Through their Jewish agents the S.S. was made aware of a change in the mood of the ghetto — Jews were again hopeful that they could escape from behind the barbed wire. The sadistic Ribe rampaged through the ghetto streets shooting at passersby right and left. He doubled the number of guards on both sides of the fence, so that it became more and more difficult to find an exit. The Jews learned, however, with the help of the people we still had inside the Jewish police, to outwit the guards.

Small, unorganized groups headed for the forest, knowing only that somewhere out there were villages known as Staroje Sielo, Lisovshtshina, Skirmontova, and that if you got there you were already in "partisan country." We even had a few "specialists" who drew crude maps of various routes to those places. People got lost on the way and were captured by the Germans. After this happened a few times we arranged for armed partisans from the Zorin brigade to "filter out" toward Minsk and try to intercept such groups. At that time, about five hundred Jews from Minsk (including older people and women with children) had reached the Zorin base.

The most spectacular arrival at the base consisted of two wagons carrying Jews rescued from the Shiroka concentration camp. They brought with them thirty rifles seized during the breakout. The organizer of this daring operation was Zyamke Gurvich. Among the people he brought out were some who had been sentenced to death. A leading part in this operation was played by Sonya Kurliandski, who was the camp kommandant's secretary. A modest, heroic young woman from Grodno, Sonya was later killed during an attempt to stage a similar escape.

From my notes, written forty years ago, I want to record here several incidents that took place during that fateful period around the end of 1942 and the beginning of 1943.

One o'clock in the morning. The sentry in my partisan unit comes in to report that near the village of Gaishtsha he has apprehended two women and they are being held there. What should he do with them? I decide to go back with him to the village to see for myself . . .

The hearts of partisans have become hard as flint. Getting a tear to fall from a partisan's eye is not one of the easiest things in the world to do. I stand opposite the two women and I can't utter a word. The tears won't stop. I am ashamed of myself for being so emotional in front of the Byelorussian partisans. Finally I control myself and ask them:

"Sisters, where are you going in the middle of this black night, with small children?"

"We're looking for Musye. Please, Comrade Commander, show us the way."

That day I wrote in my notebook:

"Everyone in the Minsk ghetto now knows about Musye, the Byelorussian woman, Maria Kulsha, from the village of Staroje Sielo. She is the representative of the ghetto underground on the road to the partisan forest. When you walk into Musye's house the bread and milk are already on the table, 'to help you keep body and soul together.' At Musye's you get directions on how to proceed deeper into the forest and find Zorin's brigade. Musye's husband had welcomed our first group headed by Nochem Feldman. Later the Nazis killed him, but Musye continues to help us with every ounce of her strength."

In the distance, in the middle of a field about ten kilometers from Minsk, we see a large group of men, women and children. We send out scouts on horseback to lead the group to a safer place — there are German garrisons all around the area. Old people and children throw their arms around us, kiss us. They had not expected this — so close to Minsk and they are already meeting partisans — and Jewish partisans at that! — who had been in the ghetto themselves. One young lad can't keep away from the horses. I remember him. Later, at the Zorin base, he was actually put in charge of the horses. Someone nicknamed him "Kolkhoznik."

Another incident. Riding along a side road we notice something moving out in the field. One of our party goes out and brings in a young boy, scared to death.

"Are you a Jewish child from the ghetto?" I ask him.

"No, Uncle, no, I'm not a Jew."

"Then why are you hiding in the field?"

The boy stammers, tongue-tied, until one of our group whispers into his ear, in Yiddish, "Are you circumcised?"

The boy blinks his eyes and we just about hear his reply:

"A little bit . . ."

His name was Mishka and he remained in the Kutuzov detachment of the Frunze brigade. After he left the forest, a Soviet army unit "mobilized" him — small as he was — to serve as one of their scouts.

Half of the Kutuzov detachment were Jews from the Minsk ghetto. At a staff meeting it was decided to set up a base in the Pegosov forest to receive the people whom Celia Klebanov brought from the ghetto. It happened once that a wagon arrived at the base with four Jewish women — accompanied by two German soldiers! This was the work of "Khashke the Baker-woman," who had become expert at smuggling flour into the ghetto. She mixed it with bran and potato skins and the result was something that only faintly resembled bread.

What had happened was this: With two wristwatches she had bribed the two German soldiers to ride out to a village with her and her three "assistants" — one of them being Celia Klebanov. Supposedly they were going into the countryside to buy food. Celia gave the driver precise directions. The wagon, with the Germans still inside it, drove straight into the arms of the Kutuzov partisans!

Another detachment of Jewish partisans from Minsk was formed and was named for Parkhomenko, a hero of the civil war. Kolya Hyman, who had been a member of one of our cells in the ghetto, was appointed Commissar of this detachment.

The number of people who came to the Zorin base from the ghetto continued to grow. Of the more than six hundred people, we selected those able to fight and formed a combat unit. A number of Jews who arrived were accepted by other partisan brigades. We kept hearing reports that our people in the diversionary groups were acquitting themselves well in battle.

Our ghetto doctors won special recognition. Chief Medical Officer of our partisan zone was Yuri Taitsh. (After he left the forest he wrote a dissertation on the performance of surgery under partisan conditions.) Dr. Zibtsiger was appointed head of the health service in the Budyoni brigade. Maria Kerson was the doctor of the new Parkhomenko detachment. Dr. Lipschitz was known throughout our partisan base as a specialist in particularly difficult cases. Dr. Dora Halperin served in the Tshkalov brigade. G. Solomnik and S. Jakubowicz, who had not yet completed their medical studies, made good use of the knowledge they had already acquired. The Zhukov brigade "stole" the former investigating judge Anna Nachiz, ("Nyuta"), of the Byelorussian court, from the Zorin base and appointed her chief aide in the special unit. (Her recollections of the Minsk ghetto are included in the *The Black Book.**)

In the spring of 1943 the partisan movement began to take on a more organized character in the western part of Byelorussia also. Haphazard activity diminished significantly. Inter-regional centers were established, headed by staff representatives of the Byelorussian partisan movement, who either rode down or were parachuted down, accompanied by heavily armed

---

* Compilation of accounts documenting the murder of 1.5 million Soviet Jews, published in English by Holocaust Library (1981).

[122]

aides, to organize diversionary or reconnaissance groups, to work among the young people, and in certain places to conduct propaganda among the local population.

In the beginning, all the partisan units consisting of people from the ghetto belonged to the Ivenietz inter-regional center. Heading this center was Grigori Dubov (G. Sidorok), who had been sent from Moscow. Before the war he had worked in this region and was known to many of the local Jews. Administering the entire partisan movement west of Minsk, near the cities that bordered on Poland prior to the war, was the Baranovitch regional center headed by Major General "Platon" (Vasili Tshernishov).

At a meeting with Feldman and the ghetto activists, we decided to take up with Platon the situation of the six hundred Jews in the Zorin brigade. Close to this region were many German garrisons and police posts. In the event of a sudden attack by the enemy, most of these Jews — unarmed men and women, children and elderly people — would not have been able to put up any resistance. The situation became especially tragic after the partisan village of Skirmontova was suddenly surrounded by S.S. units. It happened that a group of some thirty Jews had just arrived from the Minsk ghetto. All of them, together with several local farmers, were locked into barns by the S.S. and burned alive.

Platon, deeply moved by our description of the situation, decided then and there to move the entire Zorin Unit 106 into the Naliboki swamp, under the direct jurisdiction of the Ivenietz inter-regional center.

From Platon we learned, for the first time, about the large partisan brigade — close to 1200 Jews — led by Tovye Bielski. This detachment also belonged to the Ivenietz center. On the staff of this center was our very good friend Major (later Colonel) Rafail Ludvigovitsh Vasilievitsh, head of military operations. Descended from a family of Polish rebels of the 1860s who had been sentenced to a penal colony, he showed great concern for the Jews from the ghetto and helped them in every possible way. On several occasions he warned them — in time — of imminent danger.

Even though the Naliboki swamp was far from the Minsk ghetto, we still maintained contact with our people until January 1943, when our Frunze brigade suffered a disastrous blow.

It often happened to partisans: Moving their base from one forest to another, from one region to another, they sometimes revealed to the enemy where the detachment or the brigade was located. At other times an order might come from the regional staff to move to an area where the partisan forces needed strengthening.

One bitter cold night our Frunze brigade was ordered to move its base. No one on the staff had explained to us why we were leaving our caves or where we were going. We ourselves thought it might be because the secretary of one of our units had been captured by the Gestapo and tortured into giving away our position. Another guess was that we were going to join the partisans of Commander Kapusta in the Kopil region.

In any case, we came to a point where we had to cross a rail line. This required special organization, in the event we were attacked by the German guards in their bunkers. But it all proceeded as planned, without a shot being fired. Several hundred partisans, on horse-drawn sleighs, quickly crossed the rail line and stopped in a nearby forest. It was too good to be true; the whole operation had gone too smoothly.

We did not even get any advance warning from our scouts. Suddenly we were attacked by S.S. squads. We scattered in confusion. Many of our partisans were killed. The Frunze brigade fell apart. It took months for the small groups to rejoin each other at the former base, which had been destroyed by special enemy units.

The results of the Frunze defeat were felt for a long time, especially by the Jews in the brigade.

In the Forest Too — Jew-Hatred

We knew of instances where anti-Semitic language had been used during arguments with Jewish partisans. In some places commissars reacted to this in their educational talks to the units. The effects of Nazi racism, of the propaganda of the collaborationists, were evident especially among people who had escaped from Hitler's prisoner-of-war camps. Even partisans who had been out on dangerous missions alongside Jews would "entertain" themselves with anti-Jewish jokes.

In my presence — and probably to "needle" me — the young people who had been mobilized into my detachment laughed long and loud at jokes like this: "What have the various nationalities invented? The Russians — vodka; the French — champagne; the Jews — (pause) — the Jews invented the *kolkhoz*" (collective farm).

In the command post at the Ivenietz inter-regional center the political commissar was tremendously impressed with Ilya Ehrenburg's dispatches from the front, which our radio operator used to take down and type out.* Evenings, around the campfire, he would tell us what Ehrenburg had written; often he read entire articles aloud. One day I made the "mistake" of telling him that Ehrenburg was a Jew. He stopped reviewing Ehrenburg's writing for us.

Never, however, did I hear any complaints that Jewish partisans were avoiding action in combat or in diversionary operations against German troop trains. From all the brigades and detachments came reports about heroic deeds by Jewish partisans, by our young people from the ghetto, by Jewish women. The drive for vengeance against the Nazi murderers found particular expression in the activity of the Jewish *podrivniki* ("dynamiters"), as the partisans who blew up German troop trains were called. The active — often leading — participation of our people from the ghetto in the partisan detachments — Budyoni, Chapayev, May First, Tshkolov, Kalinin, 25

---

* Ilya Ehrenburg was the editor, with Vasily Grossman, of *The Black Book*, mentioned previously, written during the reign of — and suppressed by — Stalin.

Years B.S.S.R. — exposed the hollowness of the anti-Semitic charge that Jews were "sitting out the war in the hinterland."

On the contrary, when such hate propaganda was brought into our zone from the outside, it gave us the opportunity to unmask it as a diversionary trick of the enemy. One of these "tricks" led to a tragic result — for us. Near our brigade was the base of a Polish *Armia Krajowa,* Home Army legion led by Lt. Kasper Milaczewski (Lewald). (The *Armia Krajowa* had ties with the Polish government-in-exile in London.) Together we "captured" the town of Ivenietz, where 500 German troops were garrisoned. I frequently visited their staff headquarters, where Milaczewski provided me with several London periodicals, from which I gleaned fragmentary details about the destruction of Polish Jewry, the suicide of Arthur Zygelboim, his last letter, and other matters.

One day we heard the awful news that in the nearby village of Sharkovshchisna, ten Jewish partisans of the Zorin brigade had been murdered by the cavalry unit of the Polish legion, led by Sgt. Zdzislaw Narkiewicz — known as "Noc". How this had happened we learned from Ber Shimonovitsh, a Jewish partisan who had managed to escape the slaughter. Another partisan, Lyova Cherniak, from the Minsk ghetto, was seriously wounded and left for dead, but we saved him. The testimony of these two men convinced the partisan leadership to dissolve the Polish legion. The local Polish partisans were distributed among our units. The entire staff was arrested and shipped to the hinterland on the first plane that landed on our forest air-strip. Narkiewicz and his men surrendered to the S.S. units and fought with them against the partisans. After the war he was arrested in Poland and sentenced to life imprisonment. Chief witnesses for the prosecution at that trial were Lyova Cherniak and Anatole Wertheim, chief of staff of the Zorin brigade.

(The Polish Catholic weekly, *Tygodnik Powszechny*, carried an authentic description of this legion, but without a single word about the murder of the Jewish partisans by the cavalry unit, or about their switch of allegiance to the Nazis, or about the sentence of the Polish court against the collaborator Narkiewicz.)

The death of our good friend Nochem Elya Kagan was a terrible blow to all the Jewish partisans in the Frunze brigade. When we had found him hiding in a farm-house we didn't even recognize him as a Jew. With his blond, aristocratic moustache, his elongated face and his tall, erect bearing, he looked like a "real Aryan." After we talked with him for a while he acknowledged his identity. Nochem Elya the Bundist, from the shtetl of Mir, knew entire stories of Peretz from memory. Many were the times he cheered us up

[126]

with recitations from Sholem Aleichem and other Yiddish writers and poets. He knew a world of Yiddish songs. This kind, good-natured, always helpful Nochem Elya was shot in the forest by a rabid anti-Semite named Baranowski, who turned out, upon investigation, to be an agent the S.S. had sent in to spy on the partisans. The death sentence that we carried out on this murderous traitor did nothing to ease our pain. . .

There were cases of Jewish partisans being sentenced to death for negligence when the circumstances did not warrant such harsh punishment. It was a grievous hurt to us all when the entire detachment was lined up to witness the execution of Abrashka, the happy barber from Minsk.

Mazurek, secretary of the Stolpce inter-regional center, was falsely accused of being in the pay of British Intelligence. I knew Mazurek from Bialystok, where he had come with the stream of refugees from Poland in 1939. A member of the Polish section of the Writers Union and a lawyer by profession, he had proven very useful to the general staff. He spoke several languages and was able to translate the BBC broadcasts for them, but then they used this as evidence against him and shot him as a spy. We buried him not far from the staff headquarters.

Several days before Mazurek's execution we were sitting in the staff headquarters discussing the nature of the partisan press, of which I was in charge. Suddenly we heard the furious gallop of a horse. The rider leaped off his mount and burst into the cave. It was Tevl Shimanovitsh, adjutant to Major Vasilievitsh, commander of the Zhukov brigade. His swarthy face was deathly pale. We could tell he brought bad news, but for the moment it was so difficult for him to speak that we couldn't find out what had happened. All he could do was point at me and keep repeating:

"Come and you'll see!"

Before we left the headquarters I heard him mutter: "They too spill our blood. . . "

Quickly saddling my horse, I followed him. After we had gone a little distance he began telling me the story, in fragmentary phrases. We all loved Tevl Shimanovitsh, who had once been a yeshiva student and even been ordained as a rabbi. Despite this he was mobilized into the Polish army — and the calvary at that. He became an expert horseman. It wa he who taught me — relentlessly — how to handle a horse. For a whole week I could barely walk. . .

Tevl's commander, Vasilievitsh, was fond of "the rabbi," often consulting with him on military matters, particularly the "geography" of the surrounding terrain, which Tevl, having been born there, knew like the palm of his hand.

"Tevl, where are you taking me?" I demanded. "What has happened, Tevl? Tell me!"

"To the Niemen — I want you to see — not the river — but our blood that they spilled — "

What I saw on the river bank robbed me of speech.

The bodies of several Jewish women lay on the ground. It was not necessary for me to ask Tevl who had shot them. After swimming all the way across this wide river, when they finally reached the shore. . . It was not Germans who had done this — they didn't even dare step onto "our shore" unless it was part of a mass attack. These Jewish women had been murdered by our own "friends" — by other partisans.

The tears running down his cheeks, Tevl stared at me, waiting for me to tell him what to do.

To this day I cannot explain it, but this atheist of so many years could only murmur:

"Kaddish, Tevl, say Kaddish. . . "

Returning to the staff headquarters, I found both Vladimir Tsaryuk and Stieptshenko there. Tsaryuk was the official representative of the Byelorussian partisan staff. Those Jewish women had just escaped from the Nazis, I said to them. Who murdered them?

Avoiding my eyes, and speaking so softly I could barely hear him, Tsaryuk "explained":

"We were warned by reliable sources that the Gestapo had sent out a group of women to put poison in our food kettles — we're in a war — can't do anything about it now. . . "

We also ran into situations in which Jewish partisans were adversely affected and even threatened.

My good friend Major Vasilievitsh showed me the text of an order he had received from the staff of the Byelorussian movement. It spoke of partisan units that "look more like Gypsy camps — their only activity consists in getting food from the local peasants, not in fighting the Germans." Between the lines of this document I could read a threat to our large Jewish brigades, Bielski and Zorin. I shared my concern with Vasilievitsh and he confirmed it. At a meeting of the brigade staffs in the inter-regional center there had been "bad talk" about those detachments.

The Budyoni staff met and decided to advise Commanders of Bielski and Zorin of these anti-Semitic threats. We suggested that they prepare detailed reports listing the number of armed men in their detachments, the weapons they had, the date and place of their combat operations, the number of women, children and older people in their camps — mentioning the staff order to rescue the civilian population — and most important, the duties these Jews performed at the bases.

At General Platon's headquarters I learned that the "First of May" brigade had accused the Bielski detachment of systematically attacking and robbing peasants not only of food but of things that partisans didn't even need. I convinced Platon that he and Grigori Starovoytenko, editor of the partisan regional newspaper *Tshirvonaia Zviasda*, should visit Bielski's base and see for themselves. This they did, and their visit completely changed their opinion about the nature of this Jewish brigade, which was fighting for the lives of a large number of Jewish women, children and elderly people.

At the next meeting of the regional staff, General Platon made some pointed remarks: Every army must have a quartermaster corps that takes care of the daily needs of the fighting men. The Bielski brigade, which has armed, fighting units, is also the "quartermaster corps" of the partisan movement. He had seen the tailor and shoemaker workshops, the tanners — who were making leather goods under the most primitive conditions, the wurst-makers — who prepared the "untouchable reserve"* which is to be used only when a unit is under siege and cannot find any other source of food. All of these people, without exception, worked hard every day and for their labors received only a minimal, life-sustaining allotment of food.

Another danger arose from denunciations written by Jewish partisans against their own commanders. On the basis of one such denunciation the inter-regional staff began talking about dismissing Bielski and replacing Zorin with a Russian commander. They appointed as commissar for the Bielski brigade a former commander of the Kalinin brigade — his name was Shematovietz — but he turned out to be a man of integrity who defended Bielski before Commanders Dubov and Platon.

I convinced Vladimir Tsaryuk to pay a visit to the Zorin brigade. Tsaryuk, who had once been sentenced to life imprisonment in Poland, was moved to tears when he saw the young children in the camp. He proposed that we send a company of partisans to his region to collect food from the local peasants and bring it back for the Zorin brigade.

The manner in which some partisan units interpreted the Byelorussian staff order concerning people who do not take part in active combat was plainly anti-Semitic. Under the pretext that women and older people are a hindrance to the mobility of the units, they began sending Jewish partisans — including those who had been in combat — to Zorin and Bielski. In the Parkhomenko brigade — which had been organized by our people from the

---

* Russian: *Nieprikosnovienny Zapas*, shortened to "Enze" (N.Z.)

Minsk ghetto — the commander announced that in order to increase the mobility and combat readiness of the brigade, 35 partisans (some of them with wives) must leave the base and go to the Zorin brigade. The 35 men named were all Jews, some of them with combat experience. The order was effective immediately — he would not permit them to spend another night in the camp. (This was the same commander who had personally shot one of our first partisans from the ghetto (Rubenstein) for no apparent reason.)

In the Frunze brigade, three of whose four units had been formed by Jews from the Minsk ghetto, anti-Semitism took another form. After the disastrous defeat at the rail-line, months elapsed before the brigade could reorganize itself. Especially painful was the case where a group of Jews from the ghetto, whom Bronya was leading to the base, walked into a Nazi trap. We later learned that they were taken back to Minsk, where the Gestapo tortured them to divulge the name of the partisan staff representative in the ghetto. Shortly thereafter came a German "action" and we lost contact with the ghetto for a long time.

The Jewish partisans felt that defeat the hardest. Many of our comrades were killed. Only one of the four partisans with whom I had come into the forest remained — Nochem Goldsack. All the young mobilized partisans in the brigade had vanished. Then they were later seen under German guard in Koydanov, all of them but one having surrendered. I wondered about the reason for such traitorous conduct. The parents of these young people had been deported or killed in 1937 by the Soviet government. They all came from the area in which a Polish national region had been established. When I started talking with them in Polish and told them that I had studied at the university with Wilczek, Chairman of the Soviet in their region, they finally opened up. They told me what had happened to their families during the "Yezhev days." The Polish region had been liquidated together with all the Polish schools and libraries. Most of the farmers had been deported or imprisoned.

I suggested to Brigade Commissar Vautshuk that he try to reach these young people, that they still bore an open wound in their hearts. He gave me a puzzled look and advised me that I could make better use of my time to get my unit ready for the next combat operation.

The Frunze staff knew there was a great deal of dissatisfaction among the partisans with their leadership, that there was much talk about "changes." At a special meeting of the staff of all the detachments, the Brigade Commissar attempted to gloss over the reasons for the defeat at the rail-line with some high-flown rhetoric — "we all learn from our mistakes," etc. No one said a word, but it was evident that the Commissar's "explanation" had not convinced anyone.

To the visible surprise of all present, I directed several questions to Commander Subotin, rather than the speaker: How did it happen that no reconnaissance party was sent out first, while the units were resting? Why were no observation posts set up that might have prevented us from being taken completely by surprise? How did he explain the almost one-hundred-percent desertion by the young people who had been "mobilized" evidently against their will? Why had the Brigade Commissar brushed off my suggestion that he take into account their feelings about what had happened to their parents? I concluded by stating that since a defeat of this severity was unprecedented among partisans, the staff must accept responsibility for it.

As if this were not enough, Abraham Shliachtovitsh — in Warsaw they had called him "the blond Moyshe" — asked for the floor and, although his "Russian" was really a mixture of Polish and Yiddish, everyone turned to him expectantly. The brigade loved this old experienced worker who worried about everyone in the detachment and did whatever he could to help. Now he demanded that the leaders of the brigade publicly take the blame for the defeat!

Well, it didn't take long for them to "get even." Shortly after this meeting the Frunze staff came to a decision: A separate detachment would be organized for all the Jews in the brigade and it would be named for Laso, a hero of the civil war. . .

Remarkable as it may seem now, we saw this decision as an attempt to isolate us, to discredit us. "They are masters at criticizing others," Commissar Vautshuk said at a staff meeting, "now let them show what *they* can do." And he was saying this about Jews who had fought in every combat operation, who were leaders in the diversionary groups and who blew up German troop trains in the highly dangerous areas close to Minsk.

To cover up any sign that this decision was a way of settling a score with us, the order ended with the announcement that the Commissar of the Laso unit would be — Yefim Stolyarevitsh.

As Commander they appointed a Siberian named Beliakov. He was a good man, rather primitive, but with absolutely no "ethnic prejudices." It was beyond his comprehension that the brigade staff would have any anti-Jewish motives. He was a firm believer in the old adage: "*Natshalstva* (the authorities) know best." Beliakov's ability to orient himself to the terrain was amazing — a facility not given to many urban Jews. Thanks to him we avoided many a German ambush. We found a base for ourselves in the forest and began planning ways to re-establish contact with the ghetto. We had to show — all over again — what Jewish partisans could do in combat against the Nazis.

The atmosphere in our unit soon became a warmly Jewish one — including some slackening of discipline. When we sat down around the campfire during our "free hours," everyone began showing off what he remembered from the "good old days" when the world was human. Nochem Elya Kagan recited from the works of our classical Yiddish writers and from Dovid Hofshteyn and Moyshe Kulbak's poems — as well as his own. The metal-worker Meirke Rechtman, who had graduated from a CYSHO Yiddish school, told us about his famous teacher Kadya Molodowsky and recited some of her poems in his typical Warsaw dialect. Avrom Baranovitsh, from the nearby town of Ivanietz, sang entire "pieces" of the Rosh-Hashana-Yom-Kippur services like a real cantor. More than one of the partisans recalled with deep emotion the special ambience of his home during those solemn Jewish holidays.

Henyek Zucker, who had been wounded by a dum-dum bullet during our defeat, set us all an example of fortitude. Despite his serious wound, it was he who kept up our spirits after our first defeat as a separate Jewish unit. During this battle we lost Yitzhok Botvinik, one of our bravest fighters, who had gone out to meet a group from the ghetto. His mind was full of plans to organize a new unit — it was to be named for Lazar Kaganovich — but he ran into a squad of German soldiers. Together with his father and sister, who were in our detachment, we mourned our fallen comrade.

There were evenings when we gathered to bolster the spirit of our diversionary groups before they went out to place mines on railroad tracks and highways used by German transport. Many of these missions succeeded. Enemy troop trains were blown up, automobiles carrying Nazi emissaries and high German officers were wrecked. From friendly local peasants, who were the first to learn the results of these explosions, we heard about a derailment that damaged 22 railroad cars and put the line out of commission for 48 hours. Responsible for that feat was Lt. Aaron Shmushkevitsh's group. Nochem Goldsack's unit derailed a train of 40 cars carrying tanks to the German front. The same group wrecked ten cars carrying "important" passengers. Subsequently we learned that 54 Nazi officials were killed and 40 wounded in that operation. A mountain of heavy guns and other artillery weapons blocked those tracks for days.

Nochem Goldsack was a very "inventive" man. The news of one of his "inspirations" traveled overnight through the entire brigade. His "dynamiters" filled a wagon with hay, potatoes, eggs and even a few chickens. At the bottom of their "load" they buried the explosive materials. In broad daylight they drove the wagon into Minsk and stopped at the Catholic cemetery to relax their tense nerves. Then they went to work — this time a salute "in honor of" General Wilhelm Kube, arch-murderer of Byelorussia. Later that night he was killed by a partisan bomb in his bed. . .

We were the only ones who knew, however, that in all these diversionary explosions there was a *special Jewish objective*: They were arranged to take place as close to Minsk as possible. From our own experience we knew what effect it had on the Jews in the ghetto when they heard explosions so close to their "neighborhood." It strengthened their spirit of resistance when they knew that "our guys" were taking revenge on the "brown beasts." This was particularly true when, immediately following the explosions, Celia Klebanov — who had a direct hand in the "diversion" — came through the ghetto fence to lead another group into the forest. . .

In the Forest Too — Jewish Resistance

The staff of the Frunze brigade kept thinking up new ways to discredit our Jewish detachment. They kept bringing in new "materials" which allegedly showed our lack of discipline, our brutal approach toward the village population in getting food supplies, even that we spoke to each other in an incomprehensible language (Yiddish) which "proved" that we shared certain "secrets."

In order to "straighten us out," they recalled Commander Bielakov for being "too weak," a man we could wind around our little finger. In his place they appointed the commander of the Kutuzov brigade, Golitzev, who brought his partisans with him and created a much larger unit. Golitzev was a hard, obstinate man; the brigade staff was confident he would "take us in hand."

What happened was just the reverse. In contrast to the former commander, he quickly perceived the significance of the brigade staff's attitude toward us — they were "getting even" with us for having dared to hold them responsible for the disaster the brigade had suffered. "They won't get away with it — not with me!" he told me. In addition to his ambitious self-confidence, which was expressed in the frequent repetition of his favorite maxim — "This is the only authority in the forest" (pointing to his revolver) — Golitzev was quite sensitive to any kind of national discrimination. He himself belonged to one of the southern peoples and despised what he saw as Great Russian chauvinism.

After every meeting of the brigade staff he came back fuming, cursing the men who sat on their behinds all day getting drunk, doing nothing to lead the combat operations, and writing exaggerated reports about every village bridge that was blown up and every telegraph pole that was damaged. Golitzev jumped at the opportunity to leave the Frunze brigade and start an independent unit. The three of us — the Commander, the Chief-of-Staff and I — drew up a statement for the regional staff in which we described the situation in the Frunze brigade, including the inaction of the brigade staff and its discriminatory acts against the Jewish partisans.

[134]

Having decided to move in the direction of the general staff headquarters, we began evacuating our base. But we didn't get very far. We were surrounded on all sides by partisans of the other Frunze units, who had been ordered to confront us with their weapons at the ready. Golitzev, confused and disoriented, turned to me with an unspoken question in his eyes: What shall we do now?

I asked a couple of men to raise me up on their shoulders. I began to speak. "Our weapons must always and everywhere be pointed at the Hitler murderers. Are you going to fire on your own people? That would be a provocation and a crime!" Almost as soon as the first words were out of my mouth the rifles that had been pointed at us were lowered, one after the other. I then proceeded to read the statement we had prepared for General Platon, the regional commander. I had almost finished when a bullet whizzed past me and lodged in Golitzev's shoulder. The partisans surrounding us broke ranks immediately. Curses and shouts. "Grab the murderer! Get that provocateur! Put a bullet in his head!"

We never learned who fired the shot. The brigade staff carried Golitzev into their cave and did everything to help him. You could see the fear rising in their eyes: what would the regional staff do to them?

In this new situation we had no alternative but to go back to our base and wait for our commander's wound to heal. During that time the brigade staff became very solicitous of our welfare. Commander Subotin visited me frequently. But then one day I received a signal from the sole "survivor" of the mobilized young Poles. He had been under my command for a time and was then appointed Komsomol organizer for the brigade staff. What he told me — no more and no less — was that they were arranging to finish me off. During a so-called ambush, a police bullet would "take care of me." The police group would actually be a company of partisans, under orders to shoot to kill because we were really enemy agents in disguise.

It so happened that just at that time Alexander Stieptshenko, leader of the combat section of the Stolpce inter-regional center, stopped at our base on his way to his headquarters. I quickly wrote a letter to General Platon about the "death-sentence" that had been passed on me. While I was writing the letter, it occurred to me to launch a "psychological offensive" against the brigade commissar. I burst into the staff headquarters and announced, at the top of my voice:

"Platon already knows about your plan to kill me!"

In the excitement of the moment, no one apparently saw through my trick. The regional headquarters was almost fifty kilometers away. There was no way they could already have known about the brigade's plan.

The first to "recover" was Commissar Vautshuk. He tried to reassure me that there was absolutely no truth in that "rumor." On the contrary, the staff was planning to promote me and take me into their brigade . . .

Early next morning a special courier arrived with a written order from Platon: Stolyarevitch must be brought to the regional center at once.

The entire staff of the Frunze brigade was later dishonorably discharged and dispersed.

Our satisfaction over this just decision was soon replaced, however, by a feeling of growing uneasiness over the fate that hung over us all — as Jews.

At a meeting to which I had been invited by General Platon, an emissary of the central Byelorussian partisan staff reported on the situation at the various fronts and in the hinterland. In his report he discussed the changes that had been made in the composition of the Byelorussian government. With obvious relish he added: "There are no more Jews in the Byelorussian government."

So oppressive was the knowledge that anti-Semitism was still dominant "on the other side," too, the side from which our liberation was supposed to come, that I felt an ancient, smothered cry tearing out of my heart, the biblical cry of pain that I still remembered from my *heder* days.

"*Me-ayin yovo ezri?* From where shall my salvation come?"

Then a ray of hope appeared again, and this time it came directly from — Moscow. Our detachment happened to be on a tour of duty at the partisan airfield in the forest. While we were there a Soviet air-force plane landed, bringing supplies. In the baggage was a pack of fresh newspapers. By the light of the campfire we avidly read the headlines. Over one of them, we suddenly stopped. It was an appeal of the Jewish Anti-Fascist Committee addressed to the "Father of Peoples" — as was the custom in those days. But the very first words took our breath away.

I read them and reread them and couldn't believe what I was reading. The appeal began: "When the Jews received the Torah, they found a sword wrapped up inside it." One thought after another raced through my head. If — in such an important document in Moscow — they can base themselves on the Torah and refer to both the spiritual and fighting nature of the Jewish people, it could only mean one thing: the danger of Jew-hatred does not exist there . . .

My horse, which was not known for its swiftness, apparently sensed my excitement and took off in a gallop — to the Jews of the Bielski brigade, to the Jews of the Zorin brigade, to bring them the good tidings and the hope that had come to us from Moscow — through the words of our ancient Jewish sages.

On its return flight, the Soviet plane carried a letter I had written on the spur of the moment and addressed to Peretz Markish, care/of the Executive Committee of the Soviet Writers Union. In the letter I begged Markish, the Yiddish poet who was popular even among other Soviet nationalities, to ask the Byelorussian staff of the partisan movement to send us, with the next shipment of weapons, two boxes of guns for the 2000-and-more Jewish partisans from the east and from the west, who were now in the Bielski and Zorin brigades and did not have enough weapons to go around.

During my first visit to Moscow after I got out of the forest, Peretz Markish told me that he had received my letter and made the request.

But no weapons ever reached us . . .

After the Great Defeats of the Enemy

The civilian population of Minsk, primarily the shrunken number of Jews in the ghetto, felt on their own backs the heightened ferocity of the Hitlerites after their repeated defeats that followed the historic battle at Stalingrad in 1943. In an effort to counter the increased resistance and the guerrilla attacks mounted by the partisan movement, they intensified the terror still further. With the assassination of General-Kommissar Kube the occupation authorities lived in constant fear of their lives. One can see this clearly in a letter that fell into the hands of Soviet intelligence. It was written by Ernst Wesfal, director of the "Bread Factory" in Minsk, to his brother at the front.

"With us in Minsk it is one explosion after another. At night, the damn mines. The place is full of them. They blew up the generating station; there was no electricity for a week. They blew up the steam boiler in the dairy products factory. Three days ago we found several mines in the Army movie-house — luckily it was a half-hour before the picture began. Sunday evening an automobile, waiting outside the officers club for a colonel, went flying through the air. Near the water-works a locomotive blew up. Many Germans have been shot on the street and in their homes. For me, with my nerves, it's the end." (In *We Shall Tell About Minsk*, p. 50, Belarus Publishers, Russian, 1966.)

At that time there were 29 underground combat groups in Minsk, each one with three to five people. Some of the groups were sent in by partisan detachments with specific diversionary tasks; others were parachuted down. Mostly their function was to secure information about enemy forces. The activity of all these groups (their number grew to 130 during 1943) led to a steady disintegration of the German occupation apparatus. In his July 25, 1943 report to S.S. headquarters in Berlin, von dem Bach Zalewski, head of the *Einsatzkommandos*, wrote:

"In the Byelorussian administration today, chaos reigns. The administration controls only one-third of Byelorussia. The administrative apparatus itself is torn by internal power struggles, in which the purely egoistic aspects

[138]

are very obvious. Demoralization, corruption, hypocrisy of the worst sort —
these are rampant throughout."

According to information that we received both from partisan scouts and
from our own handful of couriers, a whole fleet of gassing-vans descended
on the ghetto on February 1, 1943. The Jews who were caught were sav-
agely beaten and packed into the vehicles, 80 to a van. Before the vans
reached Shashkova, a village only a half-mile from Trostynietz, all 500 Jews
were dead.

(In his letter to *Reichs-Kommissar* Lohse, July 31, 1942, Wilhelm Kube
wrote: "In all the encounters with partisans in Byelorussia it has turned out
that in the Polish and in the Soviet areas of the Kommissariat the Jews —
along with the Polish resistance movement in the south and the Soviet area in
the east — are the main support for the partisan movement. Therefore the
manner of dealing with the Jews of Byelorussia — because of the danger
threatening the general economy — is an important political problem that
must be considered not from the economic but from the political stand-
point." (Cited in previously mentioned book by A. Eisenbach)

The barbarous acts committed against the Jews of Minsk by the Germans
were repeated again and again. We felt certain that the total annihilation of
the ghetto was imminent. In June 1943 a Byelorussian named Kastus
Kurilo, wo had been a prisoner-of-war of the Germans, escaped from
Warsaw and reached our base in the forest. A native of the region around the
base, people there knew him and trusted him. From him we heard — for the
first time — about the destruction of the Warsaw Jews in Treblinka, about
the armed resistance of the Jewish Combat Organization in January 1943,
and about the uprising in April of that same year. For us this news was both a
strengthening of our pride and a portent of the approaching end of the ghetto
in Minsk.

The Nazi beast, sorely wounded and reeling from defeats on the battle-
fields, launched sporadic attacks against the partisans. During 1943 the German armies felt the full strength of the anti-Nazi movement in their own
hinterland. It was becoming more and more difficult for them to maintain
their power in the occupied territories. Day and night, partisan mines blew
up their transports on the way to the front. The Germans then set up massive
blockades of the partisan bases. In order to do this, they had to pull several
divisions from the front.

The first victims of this campaign were the peasants in the surrounding
villages. The Naliboki swamp, which is bordered on the south and west by
the Niemen River, was surrounded on all sides by regular German army
units, by companies of *Sonderkommandos*, by Lithuanian fascists and by

Cossacks from the Don who had retreated with the battered German armies. The partisans called these blockades "marathons."

The German code word for the first marathon was "*Zauberflo¨te*" (Magic Flute). The blockade around our bases in the Naliboki swamp (also later in Koydanov) lasted from the 17th to the 22nd of April, 1943. We sustained some losses, but our brigades and detachments broke through the Nazi encirclement. The blockade around our bases in July-August 1943 was larger in scope and lasted for a longer period. The German code word for this marathon was "Herman." It was led by S.S. Major-General von Gottsberg. Fifty thousand soldiers and officers combed the Naliboki swamp, shooting and shouting as if they were on a fox hunt. At that time there were almost 20,000 partisans in that area. We suffered some casualties. Our brigades split up into smaller groups that could more easily slip through the blockade.

According to German documents, during this action they burned down 150 villages. The same reports give the exaggerated figure of 130 partisans killed and 50 wounded, but they do not report how many of their own men were killed or wounded. Nor do they mention the Vlasovstes — the Russian war prisoners whom they trained in Germany especially for combat against the partisans. The case of Baranowski (cited earlier) who murdered Nochem Elya Kagan was not unique. After the blockade a new commander was appointed to lead the Rokosovsky detachment of the Zhukov brigade. He later admitted that he had been trained in a suburb of Berlin.

For us it was an occasion of great rejoicing when we learned that the staff of the Bielski and Zorin detachments had succeeded in getting all the Jews through the German lines — men, women, children and old people — without a single loss of life. When Feldman, Rosa Lipski, Nadya Shuser and I met, we evaluated this as the greatest victory scored by Tovya Bielski and Sholem Zorin, their staff and their group commanders. We saw in the results of their daring organization of Jews during the marathon the fulfillment of the task which, two years earlier, in August 1941, we had taken upon ourselves:

Keeping as many Jews as possible out of the hands of the Nazi killers.

Last Days of the Minsk Ghetto

During the July-August blockade of our forest bases, some of the new-comers from the Minsk ghetto were captured by the S.S. Tortured by the Gestapo, they revealed the addresses of the gathering points where Jews met before leaving the ghetto.

In September 1943 our guide from the ghetto to Zorin's base was 16-year-old Bronya Goldman. It was she who brought us the news that on September 1 all the men in the ghetto (except those whose hiding-places were not discovered) were taken to a camp that was under constant guard by the S.S. and police. They were taken out to work sites under heavy military escort and worked all day at gun-point.

(On June 21, 1943 a secret document was sent by Himmler to all S.S. and police commanders ordering the deportation of all employed Jews in the occupied eastern regions to concentration camps by August 21, 1943. This meant that the older people and some of the women were to be "evacuated to the east," that is, put to death. *All the ghettos were to be liquidated.* On July 13, 1943 a conference of regional ministers took place under the chairmanship of Reichs-Minister Alfred Rosenberg. In his report on Jewish problems in Byelorussia, General-Kommissar Kube requested replacements for the 16,000 Jews who were working in the auto factories in Minsk and Lide and who were scheduled for deportation at an early date. See A. Eisenbach, p. 377.)

Alexander Pechorsky, who was a prisoner in the Shiroka concentration camp and later led the uprising in the Sobibor death camp, reports:

"In September 1943 the Germans hurriedly began evacuating all the Jews who were still left in the Minsk ghetto. Transports of 2000 people were taken from the ghetto to the camp on Shiroka Street and from there to other destinations . . . . On September 18th the Jews were lined up in the yard. It was four o'clock in the morning. Shrouded in darkness, their bundles in hand, people stood in line for the 300 grams of bread issued for the trip. The yard was filled with people, but you could not hear anyone talking. Children clung to their mothers in fear. That morning no one was beaten, no one was

[141]

scalded with boiling water, no one was set upon by the dogs. Kommandant Waks, toying with his whip, announced:

"'You will all be taken to the railroad station. You are going to Germany to work. Hitler has found it possible to spare the lives of those Jews who want to work honestly for Germany. You are going with your families and you may take with you your more valuable belongings.'

"The women and children were driven to the station in automobiles. The men walked. On the way, we passed the ghetto. When the Jews there saw us, they threw bread and other food to us over the fence. You could hear people saying goodbye to each other; some were crying. Everyone knew what awaited them . . .

"On the fifth day, in the afternoon, the train stopped at a remote, little-used station. On a white sign, in big Gothic letters, was the single word SOBIBOR. To the right was a forest, to the left stretched a barbed-wire fence — three strands of barbed wire, three meters high." (Alexander Pechorsky, *Uprising in Sobibor*, pp. 5-6, State Publishing House, Der Emes, Moscow, 1946.)

So we know that in September 1943 there were still Jews left in the Minsk ghetto. On October 1st the last 2000 Jews in the ghetto were still trying desperately to escape. Bronya told us that even the criminals in the "Operative Group" were in a panic, even though they were supposedly still in charge of the Judenrat, the Labor Exchange and the Jewish Police. One of them, a man named Singer, assured us (through an intermediary) that he wanted to "atone for his sins," that he would do whatever we ordered him to. He actually did forewarn us of raids by Epstein's "operatives" on suspicious apartments and "malinas." He brought us letters from Jews who had been arrested by Rosenblatt and kept in the jail-house. We instructed Mira Strongin, in the Labor Exchange, to do whatever she could to split the Operative Group and to try to persuade some of them to join one of our partisan units in the forest.

We were successful in getting Ginsberg to leave the ghetto — the Jews feared him as much as they did the German police. Mira Markman, Misha Kagan and Abramchik, of the Operative Group, also left the ghetto. The head of the inter-regional partisan staff (G. Dibov) instructed us to have these traitors tried by partisans from the Minsk ghetto itself. The unanimous verdict — "For dogs, a dog's death!" — was accompanied by the recommendation not to waste bullets on them but to give them each a cup of poison . . .

Another four of the "Operatives" were preparing to come into the forest — Meir Segalovitsh, his son, Shulman and Rubin. At the last moment, however, they were "betrayed" by one of their gang named Bierkowski. All of them were shot before they could leave the ghetto.

We were unable to inveigle Epstein and Rosenblatt to come out to us. Up to the last moment they helped the *Einsatzkommandos* complete the liquidation of the ghetto.

At that time I was assigned to the staff of the Stolpce inter-regional partisan center (by order of General Platon). Our base was located south of the Naliboki swamp, about seventy kilometers from the Bielski and Zorin bases. It was difficult to maintain daily contact with them, but we had agreed that whenever Bronya Feldman went into the ghetto to bring out our people, we would meet in Zorin's headquarters to get the latest information and decide, on the spot, what to do next. That was the situation at the end of October 1943.

When I got to Zorin's headquarters, everyone was there. One look at the faces of Commander Sholem Zorin, Commissar Haim Feygelman and Chief-of-Staff Wertheim and I felt as though my heart had stopped beating. To my almost hysterical question: "Bronya didn't make it?" — Zorin quietly asked his adjutant to call her in.

She was barely recognizable. Her usually smiling young face was shrouded in deep sorrow. She looked at me helplessly, barely able to speak.

No — she had not been able to get into the ghetto this time — there was no ghetto left in Minsk — only smoke, heavy smoke, black soot everywhere — she could hear the sound of machine-guns, rifles, grenades —

On the way back she met several people who had managed to escape. She had brought them into the forest.

These Jews told us:

"At dawn on October 21st, it began. What was left of the ghetto was surrounded on all sides. To the accompaniment of their usual bellowing — 'Raus! Raus!' — the Nazis drove people from their homes half-undressed. The advance unit consisted of Epstein, Rosenblatt and the rest of that gang, shouting 'Jews, there's no use hiding, we'll find you anyway!' People they found hiding were often shot on the spot. The dead lay in the streets. The barking of dogs smothered the groans of the wounded. The ghetto of the hundred thousand Jews of Minsk no longer existed."

When we recovered from this shattering news, Zorin's staff decided to send out immediately several men — on horseback and on foot — to intercept any Jews who might be lost on the roads around Minsk. That same day, ninety people were brought to the partisan village and later to Zorin's base. A few others, hidden in their ghetto "malinas" stayed there till nightfall and then set out toward the east, where the number of partisan detachments was greater at that time.

How many Jews escaped that last massacre we did not know. Later, isolated Jews would sometimes come into the forest. A very small number — perhaps ten — survived in their hiding-places until the day of liberation.

The Eulogy and the Oath

The order from the Zorin staff was: Everyone without exception, young and old, women and children, and also those Jews who had just arrived, whose clothing still showed the faded outlines of the yellow patch — everyone must line up for the collective eulogy to the slaughtered ghetto of Minsk.

"More than two years ago, in August 1941, we appealed from our underground to the Jews in the Minsk ghetto with the warning, 'Ghetto means death! By every means possible, break down the fence around the ghetto!' By the end of the first year of occupation we had opened a way to the partisan forest. Now we must bring you the dreadful news:

"The ghetto no longer exists.

"There are no more Jews in that city where entire generations of Jews shaped its Jewish look, its Jewish character, and molded its way of life with their blood and their sweat.

"They no longer exist, the Jews of Minsk, who inscribed their names in the history of our people with their pioneering role in establishing and developing all the social movements that produced fighters for our national and social liberation.

"They no longer exist, the Jews of Minsk, who contributed so much to our national and cultural advancement. In the streets and by-ways of Minsk you can no longer hear the sound of our Yiddish speech.

"They no longer exist, the Jews of Minsk, whose sons and daughters, at the end of the last century, helped to consolidate the militant freedom-forces of all of Russia. The Nazi barbarians destroyed the wooden building in Minsk where Jewish workers helped to organize the first conference of the Russian labor movement.

"They no longer exist, the Jews of Minsk, the city which saw the rise of the movement that we know so familiarly as 'the Minchukes.'

"No more Jewish Minsk, whose sons and daughters fought on the barricades in 1905 to bring down the walls of that enormous ghetto known as the Pale of Settlement.

"No more Jewish Minsk, where thousands upon thousands of our people joined the armed struggle against the pogromchiks at the time of the civil war, when they organized special Jewish militia units.

"It no longer exists, the city which witnessed the flowering of Yiddish art and literature.

"And there is no longer any hope of saving it. We are all orphans, we, the last Jews of the ghetto . . ."

I could not finish. The weeping grew louder and louder. And at this point, little Felek, Rosa Lipski's young son, began tugging at my leg, pleading:

"Enough, Uncle Yefim, enough talking — let's sing, instead."

But before we started the singing, which sounded more like a collective kaddish, came the stubborn oath of the Jewish partisans:

"If there are no more Jews, then *we* shall be the Jewish people!

"Vengeance for our slaughtered families! Vengeance against the brown-shirted murderers! Each day, each hour, repay them with our burning hatred and our unceasing struggle!"

Jewish Blood on the Threshold of Liberation

The staff of the Stolpce inter-regional partisan center knew very well that we were facing extremely critical days. On June 23, 1944, early in the morning, Lyuda, our radio operator, ran into our staff so excited she could only manage to get out three words:

"BAGRATYON is coming!"

When she calmed down she told us that she had just heard a news item: That morning the all-out offensive against the German armies had begun. The name of the offensive was BAGRATYON. Along the entire front — north, east, south — moving toward the capital of Byelorussia — Minsk.

At our meeting that same morning we divided amongst ourselves the duty of bringing this news to all the brigades and detachments, along with the order to stay on full alert, bearing in mind that the surrounded Nazi military units would try to retreat through our forests. We must not allow them to do that. We must pursue them and wipe them out. Relentlessly.

Without reporting to Vladim Tsaryuk, representative of the Byelorussian partisan center, I mounted my white dray-horse and spurred him on to his maximum speed, so that I could warn the Jewish bases in time.

This warning, however, did not prevent us — the Jews from the Minsk ghetto — from paying with our blood on the eve of leaving the forest. Unit 106 posted guards on all sides and made certain the children and the older people would be protected.

And yet . . .

These were not solitary Germans fleeing for their lives. This was a large company of S.S. cutthroats. They ran into our armed guards and started shooting, hitting Commander Zorin himself. And here, at the last moment, not far from the place they had been defending with all their strength, so that they could save the lives of hundreds of Jews, some of our fighters were killed. Commander Zorin, one of the first partisans from the Minsk ghetto, was so badly wounded that it became necessary to amputate his leg.

[147]

Among the dead I recognized my fellow-townsmen, Dr. Patshutski and his wife. For years they had lived on the same street with my parents. One day, when I spoke at a gathering of Jewish partisans, they recognized me. We talked about the future. They were so hopeful about returning to a normal life . . .

Returning to our liberated native city, we walked like mourners following a coffin. No longer did we have any hope of perhaps meeting someone there that we knew. The casualties we had suffered, while all the other partisan detachments came out without a scratch, oppressed the spirit of the Jews who, in the 160th partisan unit had regained the confidence that they would live to see the day of vengeance against the Nazi enemy.

Hayim! We Live!

This time it was different than in the ghetto, where we had to depend on information from the Judenrat and our Nazi "overseers" to learn how many Jews were still alive after each German action. Now we did the counting ourselves, on the basis of information from the returning Jewish partisans and from people (most of them women) who had lived among the Byelorussians with "Aryan documents."

From the Byelorussian central partisan staff, which was now headquartered outside of Minsk, we received an announcement that on July 16, 1944, in the large Hippodrome in Moscow, there would be a mass meeting to celebrate the liberation. Following that, there would be a march of 30,000 partisans. On the accompanying list of partisan brigades and detachments that were coming to participate in the parade, the partisans of our center were not included. The reason: We must stay on the alert and not allow the beaten armies of the enemy to hide and regroup in the swamp. We must continue to be in combat readiness at all times. We must help the Soviet army units that were now on the offensive.

We were invited, however, to send two partisans who would represent all the brigades and detachments of the Stolpce inter-regional center. Appointed to represent us were Yanka Bril, a young Byelorussian writer and former soldier in the Polish army who had fought against the invading Nazis around the Baltic Sea — and Yefim Stolyarevitsh.

As had happened three years earlier, when Hitler invaded Byelorussia, I found myself again walking the length of Minsk's Moscow Street which was piled high with heaps of rubble, except that now the heaps were hills. For a moment I paused at the building that had been the home of illegal political activists from Byelorussia. But only for a moment.

In the Byelorussian staff headquarters we were received in a very friendly manner and told that there would be a place for us on the reviewing stand during the parade. Romanov, head of the cadre department on the Byelorussian staff, whom I had known in Bialystok, greeted me like a long-lost brother. But his joy suddenly evaporated when I asked him if someone in his unit could complete accurate figures for us on the number of Jews in the Byelorussian partisan movement, according to each region, but especially from Minsk. Scowling, he replied:

"We don't keep statistics according to national origin. . . "

Which was absolutely untrue. In a report later released by the Byelorussian staff, the national origin was given — for all except Jews. The Jewish partisans were "squeezed in" among a number of tiny national groups under: OTHER.

Minsk in those days was one tremendous partisan camp. At every step one met armed men in the most bizarre dress, even in German uniforms taken from prisoners, but with the unmistakable partisan symbol — the red ribbon on the cap. In the heart of the city, among the ruins, grazing on the weeds and crabgrass, were the partisan horses. High in the clear summer sky floated the smoke of partisan campfires. On sticks and iron rods hung large scorched kettles, in which partisans — as if they were still in the forest — were cooking something "to tide them over." And in accordance with partisan custom we sat down among a group of men completely unknown to us and stuck our inseparable companions — our spoons — into the common kettle of stew.

Although less than a tenth of the 370,000 partisans of Byelorussia in the 1100 detachments came to the parade, it was still a thrilling sight: What a mighty force we represented! It was this army of relentless avengers that — by the end of 1943 — had regained control of 60% of Byelorussia and in twenty regions established full partisan authority. It was this partisan army and its "war on the railroad tracks" that completely disrupted rail communications on the night of August 3, 1943, rail connections that the enemy on the northeastern front used to transport its reserves, its weapons and its ammunition. On that one night, 42,000 rails "flew up in the air."

And on June 20, 1944, two weeks before the beginning of the "BAGRATYON" offensive of the Soviet armies, hundreds of thousands of rails again flew in the air and we gave them a send-off with brightly colored tracer bullets. That was the night that the lines between Minsk and Orsha, Polotsk and Molodetshna, Gluboks and Vilna, were totally disrupted — and most importantly, between Minsk and Bryansk — all of these points extremely important for the enemy's middle front.

(In one of his lectures, Professor Jehoshophat Harkavi allowed that this large number of partisans would have been in the regular army if they had been more "battle-worthy." I beg to differ with the honorable professor. A regular army would not have been able to demoralize and defeat the administrative power in the occupier's hinterland, disrupt his communications and report daily to its general staff on every movement of the enemy. By means of its "network" the inter-regional partisan staff on which I served was able to issue daily intelligence reports on the Nazi administration and their army. And this does not even take into account the tremendous significance of the partisan movement as a political-moral factor in inspiring the entire population of the occupied regions to resist the enemy.)

I introduced Yanka Bril, my co-delegate at the parade, to my old comrades, the Byelorussian writers Maxim Tank, Philip Piestrakh, Pantchenko and others. (Later, after having read his partisan novels, they recognized him as a talented writer.) Then I took a walk in the neighborhoods beyond the center of the city, where thousands of temporary homes had been set up. Here many of the Jews lived whom I had known in the ghetto and the forest.

Often, when we embraced, we could not utter a word, so deep was the joy of having survived, of having "outlived the enemy," of having returned to our native city that now lay in ruins.

With Nochem Feldman, who was attending as Commissar of a large partisan detachment, I found it impossible to talk at all. "Let's wait until later, after the parade," he suggested. When it was proposed, however, that we all visit the graves of our families in the area of the ghetto, we walked silently to the destroyed streets of the ghetto, mute witnesses to the murder of the last Jews left behind the barbed wire fence. Still standing was the Judenrat building, its doors and windows gaping. Also, the Labor Exchange and Jubilee Square, with its trees lying on the ground as if felled by a storm.

Still there was the Jewish cemetery, with open or barely covered graves containing the remains of Jews who had been shot by the Nazis. Still there — but without any sign as to what it was — was the place where 5000 Jews had been murdered on Purim 1942. The ghetto hospital — with my hiding-place in the boiler-room — was still there, too.

On the way back, Feldman and I agreed to meet after the parade to discuss what had to be done next.

None of us had ever seen a parade like this before. Brigade after brigade, men in part-civilian and part-military clothing, carrying the most diverse kinds of weapons, some of them "hand-made" with partisan inventiveness.

I looked hard at each detachment that marched by, searching — and often finding — Jews with whom I had been close friends. Many a hand in the ranks went up happily in a gesture of recognition. At one point I could not restrain myself and called out:

"Hayim!"

It was Haim Aleksandrovitsh, marching by the side of "Diadia Vasya"

(Voromanski), pioneer of the partisan movement and my good friend from the Minsk ghetto.

As I called out "Hayim," everyone on the platform — the generals with their bemedalled chests, the government leaders — turned to stare at me, some in surprise, some in anger, some with a sarcastic grimace. The chief of the partisan general staff, Pantileimon Ponomarenko, practically impaled me with his suspicious glare. As it turned out later, he never did forget my unrestrained, enthusiastic cry of "Hayim!"

Around the Last Partisan Campfire

After the parade, most of the participants headed for the "partisan village" near the Byelorussian staff headquarters. People had business to take care of there — primarily to obtain the documents showing that they had served in this great people's movement of revenge against the Germans — as well as to pick up their well-deserved medals and decorations that had been awarded to them while they were still in the forest.

At every step we met other Jews. The joy of meeting all these people was tempered by concern. What next? No families, no homes, no jobs. What could one do when one's only possession was a rifle or an automatic pistol.

The first thing we did was to get a campfire going in the open field. The cool breeze was pleasant and the crackling of the dry branches was reminiscent of the days we had spent together. We still acted like partisans — we had not yet become anything else. We talked about the past, about how we left the ghetto, about our friends on both sides of the ghetto fence who had perished. In a most natural way, the talk then went to battle experiences in the forest. People would often interject — "that's exactly how it happened with us!"

I could not take my eyes off the sun-bronzed young face of Boris Haimovitsh. He was the only one left of the four friends with whom — on that Sunday in August 1941 — I had begun the chapter of the resistance organization in the Minsk ghetto. And he was the first one to go out into the forest. He remembered much about those early days and about our first losses. Gone was Notke Wainhoyz, whom some of the Minskers recalled from the days when he was editor of the Yiddish children's newspaper and was always surrounded by youngsters whose Yiddish songs rang out in the streets of Minsk, much to the delight of the Jews. Gone was the chubby Jascha Kirkayeshto and his "Odessa Yiddish." How painful to think about Misha Gebelev. How many of the partisans around that campfire — and the crowd was getting bigger all the time — were led out of the ghetto by that fearless Misha . . .? There were a few men here who had gone to the same school with the incredibly heroic Emma Radova. Haim Alesandrovitsh

[153]

recalled how Motya Pruslin and Meir Feldman fell during a surprise attack by an S.S. group. Fedka Shedletski — our first courier of the forest brigade — was quiet and pensive, his chest already decorated with his awards.

We sat around the fire far into the night, unwilling to break up the talk of Jewish achievements in the tenacious fight against the destroyers of our people. The name "Diadia Vasya" was already known to us in the ghetto early in 1942. He was the first partisan commander (his name was Voromanski) who had held out his hand to us in those most difficult days. So it was natural for our people who organized partisan Unit 406 to join Diadia Vasya's detachment. It was he also who helped them keep "a special Jewish account."

For example, when the detachment went out to attack the Nazi garrison in the town of Miadiel (Vileika region), they also had the assignment of liberating the Jews in the ghetto there. But what were we to do with the older people, the women and children? Commander Diadia Vasya thought of a bold plan: to lead them, under partisan escort, to the other side through a "hole" in the front lines. His plan worked. And that was only a beginning. Thousands of Jews — mainly from the Minsk ghetto — were saved this way, among them our comrades Dina Madeisker and Lena Maiselis.

Someone whispered to Boris: "Show us, show us what it says there!" By the light of the campfire the partisan read the "testimonial" issued by the staff of the 208th partisan regiment, which stated that "Boris Faivelovitsh Haimovitsh, who set an example of heroism and daring, took part in forty partisan battles." I felt my own chest bursting with pride as I looked at Boris, his head lowered shyly — the proud head of the first partisan of the Minsk ghetto.

I knew the name of Hirsh Dobin, the Yiddish writer, before the war. Now partisans were telling about him — how he managed to work not only with his rifle but with his pencil. And how he cheered up the partisans with his satirical series of forest sketches called (in Russian) *"Knishka Malyshka — Fashistam Krishka"* ("The Tiny Book — An End to the Fascists!")

Shimon Lapidus was already an elderly man, but he kept pace with the younger men when his son Israel Lapidus left the ghetto with a group to set up our own partisan base in the Kolodin forest. Shimon played a very useful role on that mission. In the forest he felt a lot younger as he told his fellow partisans how he and others like him fought in the civil war in 1919. He taught the younger partisans the basic essentials of forest life: "Always keep your eyes and ears wide open and your bullets dry and ready."

And when Commander Israel Lapidus selected sixty men for a mission on the highway from Puhowitsh to Stari Dorogi, Shimon was one of them. And it was he who kept cautioning the young hotheads: "Patience, men, wait patiently and stay out of sight . . ." And they waited patiently, until the very last moment. Nine trucks, carrying an *Einsatzkommando* unit on its way to "wipe out" partisans were themselves wiped out instead. Israel Lapidus's partisans surrounded the Nazis with such a ring of fire that they could neither advance nor retreat. The Jewish partisans fought at such white-heat that they finished off the murderers with their own bare hands.

Old Shimon jumped up on a truck and swung his rifle butt around like a club on the heads of the bewildered Nazis. As if he were the Commander himself, he kept urging on the partisans: "Pay them, youngsters, pay them back for the ghetto, for Tutshinka!" Seventy-four fascists died in that encounter. Joseph Yankelevitsh choked some of them to death with his bare hands. Abraham Holiavski split open a few heads with the butt of his revolver — "It was a pity to waste good bullets," he laughed. "We took eight of them prisoner," Shimon added, "and when they heard the sound of our Minsk Yiddish, their rotten blood froze."

Lazer Losik told us how "on his own initiative" he sent a peasant, whom he knew well, to bring his mother and sister out of the ghetto — and as many Jews and guns as he could. The first and second missions were successful. The third was not . . .

Around the campfire, Yitzhok Mindel's story sounded like an anecdote, but it really happened, at the start of the "marathon."

"A German plane flew over our heads and dropped a bomb right at my feet. It was a real miracle. The bomb could have killed scores of partisans in the newly organized Parhomenko brigade. But it didn't go off. So what did our guys do? Haim Bernstein, Haim Dvoskin and Zuckerman, our trio of dynamiters, decided to send the bomb back where it came from. They concealed it on the road near Poldorazhia (Ivinietz region). Result: Thirty fascists, on their way to attack a partisan base, were killed by their own bomb, returned to them by Jewish partisans . . ."

We could have sat there this way three days and three nights, and kept adding wood to the fire, and still not have told each other everything the Jews who broke through the ghetto fence did to wreak vengeance on the murderers of our people.

We did not know yet what the total figures were, but we did know for certain that the following partisan detachments were formed, on our initiative, in the ghetto and in the forest, with the help of the combat organization in the Minsk ghetto, of many hundreds of its members and sympathizers, and of the resistance movement in occupied Minsk, as well as of the partisan commanders who were ready to meet us halfway:

Partisan Detachment 406 (later united with the heroic detachment of Diadia Vasya).

The Fifth Detachment, Kutuzov, (of the 2nd Minsk partisan brigade).

The Budyoni Detachment (of the Ponomarenko brigade).

The Dzerzhinski Detachment (of the Frunze brigade).

The Sergei Lasos Detachment (later united with the Kutuzov Detachment).

The Parhomenko Detachment (of the Chapayev brigade).

Detachment 106 (Zorintses), comprised of more than 600 Jews of the Minsk ghetto.

This incontestable total of direct, organized, mass participation of the Minsk Jews in armed partisan combat against the Nazis was given by us to the Byelorussian general staff of the partisan movement, who confirmed it. We also provided them with the facts about the active participation of the Minsk ghetto underground in many diversionary acts which resulted in the deaths of hundreds of Hitlerites and the destruction of enterprises producing materials for the German army.

Instead of Sympathy and Help —
Hatred and Threats

During those first days after liberation we met frequently, as a committee. Nochem Goldman, Boris Haimovitsh, Haim Aleksandrovitsh, Rosa Lipski and I met for the last time. We were, after all, no longer in the ghetto, where we had felt responsible for the fate of the Jews behind the barbed wire fence. We were no longer in the forest, where we had been able, even without legal recognition, to do something on behalf of the Jews in the ghetto. We were now under the authority of Soviet norms, which deny people the right to initiative of any sort, without the prior agreement and permission of the leading Party and government bodies. For a meeting of this kind, which adopted independent decisions, we could be charged with the worst of crimes — fractionalism, and nationalist fractionalism to boot!

And — a short time later — that is what actually happened. The accusation came from the highest office in Byelorussia — the Prime Minister and First Secretary of the Central Committee of the Communist Party.

At our final meeting, then, we — the former leaders of the combat organization in the Minsk ghetto — decided:

(1) To mobilize the maximum number of Jewish partisans possible for the purpose of gathering information from all the brigades and detachments concerning the number of Jews who had come into the forest from the ghetto, either in organized groups or as individuals. Boris and Haim were responsible for the eastern zones; Nochem, Rosa and I for the western zones. We would try to get help in this effort from whatever sources we deemed necessary.

(2) To try in every possible way to speak with leading people in the Communist Party and the government in order to make them aware of what had happened with the Jews in the Minsk ghetto, including Jewish participation in the anti-Nazi resistance, and of the situation of those who had returned from the forest and from their hiding-places. And to request help for them in making the transition to a normal life.

[157]

The census was taken by scores of Jewish partisan groups. Several of them were even able to go back into the forest to the brigades that had not taken part in the parade. We had no illusions whatsoever that this kind of census would record precisely the number of Jews who broke out of the ghetto, or the numbers that had remained alive after months and years of fighting. Nevertheless it did give us a certain picture of the results of the collective and individual response to our basic appeal early in the occupation: "Ghetto means death! Break down the fences of the ghetto!"

The "bottom line" of the reckoning looked something like this:

From the Minsk ghetto, over a period of 25 months — four in 1941, through all of 1942 and nine in 1943 — close to ten thousand Jews, including women, children and old people, had managed to get to the forest. They had done this through the ghetto combat organization, or with the help of the all-Minsk resistance center, or through various partisan detachments. There were also individuals and independent groups. We were unable to get an accounting of the Jews who survived on the "Russian side."

With regard to our second task — to help the Jews who had returned — we ran into a stone wall. In accordance with our decision, I asked for a meeting with V. Zakurdaiev, Secretary of the Central Committee of the Byelorussian Communist Party, who was in charge of social assistance. Getting an appointment with a Party or government leader had always been very difficult. Often you would have to wait a long time, and this was especially true now, with all the difficulties they were having in ccating the most elementary conditions for a normally functioning government. Imagine my surprise, then, when they promised me that the Secretary of the Central Committee would see me the very next morning!

I left that meeting sorely depressed. Haim Alexandrovitch described my feeling with the familiar Yiddish saying: "You went to claim your inheritance and had to pay for the burial. . . " (The details of that meeting can be found in my book, *"Where Are You, Comrade Sidorov?"* pages 232-253).*

Instead of listening to what I had to say, Zakurdaiev did not even allow me to speak about our most urgent problems. At the time, I was still at a loss to understand why they had given me this appointment with such alacrity. For a moment I even thought it was done out of sympathy for the great tragedy of our people and that they were ready to help us. . . It turned out to be exactly the reverse.

Zakurdaiev asked me to tell him, in minute detail, how it came about that the Minsk combat organization was formed, who the organizers were, what

---

* *Vu Bist Du, Tovarich Sidorov?*, published by Peretz Farlag, Tel Aviv, 1975.

[158]

differences of opinion there might have been among us. And as I spoke, he took copious notes.

When I got to the essential purpose of my visit — the events in the ghetto, the role of the ghetto underground, the situation of the Jews who were returning from the forest — he grew more and more agitated and impatient. They had no place to live, I told him. Even if their old apartments had remained intact, there were other people living there now. They had nothing to wear, they had no money for food. I also mentioned the need to re-create their Jewish cultural life as a way of demonstrating that the Nazi barbarians had not succeeded in their aim of destroying the culture of the Jews.

The longer I spoke the clearer it became that the Secretary was not even listening. He wasn't even looking at me. When I finished, he fixed his eyes on me like spears and, by way of reply, asked me a question that so unnerved me that I couldn't even get up out of my chair. After all I had just told him, he asked me a question that actually constituted a statement: "Of all the peoples, nationalities and tribes in the U.S.S.R., why is no one hated as much as the Jews?"

I didn't say another word. Zakurdaiev apparently saw in my face the effect of his anti-Semitic "question" and tried to soften it by proposing that I write down "everything" I had told him.

After all this, we nevertheless decided to prepare a document detailing what had happened in that ghetto of 100,000 Soviet Jews and what the ghetto underground had done, including a list of 150 of its active members. W also described the difficult situation of the 5000 Jews who had returned either from active duty with the partisans or from their hiding-places on the Russian side and in various nearby villages. We concluded with proposals for financial assistance and for restoring Jewish cultural life. We sent this "memorandum" to the Secretariat of the Central Committee, and in order to avoid any reason for suspicion that there was "a Jewish fraction" out there somewhere, the only signature on it was mine.

Very shortly afterward I received an invitation to meet with Comrade Malin, Secretary of the Central Committee. Like Zakurdaiev, he seemed interested mainly in the organizational period of the all-Minsk resistance center, its leading members, their activities and their internal disagreements (expecially in regard to the "Military Council").*

And again, like Zakurdaiev, he had no interest whatever in what happened inside the Minsk ghetto, or in the pioneer role of the ghetto under-

---

* Some Soviet historians try to rehabilitate the "Military Council" despite the fact that its leaders broke completely under Gestapo interrogation.

ground in creating the Minsk combat center, or in the urgent problems facing the thousands of Jews who had returned. Again the answer was the same:

"Prepare a *dokladnaya zapiska* — a bill of particulars — and wait for an answer."

My friends — Byelorussian writers — cleared up the mystery for me — why the Secretaries of the Central Committee had received me so quickly and why they were so interested in how the combat organization in Minsk was formed:

First, of all the people who had been involved in the creation of the first and second resistance centers in Minsk, I was the only one who had survived the war. (Years later my documentation was used by historians and writers of *belles-lettres*.) Second, I learned that early in 1942, when Moscow heard about the establishment of the Minsk combat organization and its activity, it was regarded as the work of — provocateurs! This shameful "explanation" was supposed to excuse the panicky flight of the Byelorussian Party and government leaders, who not only did nothing to evacuate the population, but who didn't even leave any official representatives behind to organize resistance against the German occupier of their capital. And since — without the help of the Communist Party Central Committee — a resistance center was nevertheless organized, inspired in great measure by the underground Jewish organization that had already appeared in the ghetto, and since the Minsk city center was headed by an unknown young man with the pseudonym of Slavek-Pobiedit, how could it have been anything else but the work of "provocateurs"?

As the sole survivor, I was the one that had to be "interrogated," so that fourteen years later, in July 1960, they could publish an official document, prepared by the Institute for Party History of the Central Committee and the Historical Institute of the Academy of Science, a work which deals with the activity of the underground combat organization in Minsk and is based on eyewitness testimony.

Insofar as the ghetto is concerned, the preface of this official document says: "In the ghetto, which the Hitlerites set up in the area of Ostrovski, Niemiga, Republikaner, Abuvna, Opanski, Sukha, Tatarski Streets and Jubilee Square, the Soviet citizens of Jewish nationality were totally destroyed." Concerning the combat organization of the ghetto, the document says that "in the ghetto group were: M. L. Gebelev, M. L. Yekeltshik, M. M. Pruslin, H. M. Pruslina, H. D. Smolar ("Yefim," "Skromni," 'Stolyarevitsh"), N. L. Feldman and others." And that's all.

Although my materials and my book about the Minsk ghetto were used in

[160]

this document, when they came to describe the activity of various people, they totally ignored the role and the self-sacrificing acts of the ghetto underground. This document was written during a period of heightened anti-Semitism in the Soviet Union, including Byelorussia.

In the meantime there were certain developments that threatened our first independent Jewish steps in Minsk.

A group of Jewish partisans and war invalids came to me with a question: "What are we going to do about the anti-Semites who are running wild in Minsk? They insult Jews, they beat and rob the few Jewish women who are trying to sell some of the valuables they had left in the care of honest neighbors — they simply need the money to buy food."

The answer to that question could only be: "Resistance! Don't tolerate it!" No sooner said than done. Jewish partisans and Jewish war invalids succeeded in calming down the anti-Semitic gangs.

Quite by accident I met the Yiddish writer Yirmiahu Drucker on the street. He was still in the army. We had met when I was editor of *Di Yunge Gvardie*, a Yiddish youth newspaper in Kharkov. From him I learned that Isaac Plotner and Hirsh Kamenietski, Yiddish poets, had returned from the east. During the Yezhov purge in 1937-38 they had barely escaped with their lives.

The four of us met and decided to arrange a Yiddish literary morning. I was to prepare a lecture on Soviet-Yiddish literature in the fight against Hitler Fascism. Plotner and Kamenietski would read some of their poems. (Drucker, as a member of the Soviet armed forces, thought it better not to participate.) We were given permission by the Director of the main library, part of which had escaped destruction, to use a room in his building.

It was the first Yiddish cultural event since liberation. A large crowd came, eager "to hear a Yiddish word." Everything went according to plan, except for a brief word from an air-force major who held up his empty sleeve and said:

"Although I am an invalid, I could still be a flyer for our Jewish homeland — Palestine!"

News of both these events — our resistance against the anti-Semitic bullies and the "speech" of the Jewish pilot — quickly reached the ears of the highest Soviet government officials.

At a third meeting with a party official which took place late one evening, this time with the "Boss" of Byelorussia himself — Prime Minister and First Secretary of the Communist Party's Central Committee, P. Ponomarenko — Plotner, Kamenietski and I heard words that both my friends, the Soviet-

Yiddish poets, intrepreted to mean that a sentence of death had been passed on us that night.

The Prime Minister listened patiently to my words about the situation of the returning Jews, about the need for a sympathetic approach to these people who had suffered so much and who were now without families, without shelter, without jobs, about the need to encourage them and to comfort them with the artistic creations of Yiddish writers and actors.

This time, however, there was no suggestion that I "write it all down." Our "documentation" was well known to Ponomarenko; during this meeting it led him to accuse me of "nationalistic narrowness." But that was the mildest of the accusations. From Ponomarenko we heard words that night that were full of threats, accusations and hostility:

"It was you people who organized Jewish gangs to beat up war invalids! It was you who organized a Jewish nationalist meeting with Zionist speeches! We'll soon put a stop to that. . . "

And although at that time I was not as certain as my Soviet friends that Ponomarenko had decreed a death sentence for us, I was nonetheless gripped by uneasiness about our fate. (Four years later Plotner and Kamenietski were arrested. Soon after their "rehabilitation" they both died in Minsk.)

As quickly as I could — in that difficult winter of 1944-45 — I wrote a book about the Minsk ghetto and took it to Emes Publishing House in Moscow. As I was telling my story to Shachna Epstein, secretary of the Jewish Anti-Fascist Committee, and my old friend Itsik Feffer, I got the impression that they didn't take too seriously the threats of the Boss of Byelorussia. After I gave them the documents about the Minsk ghetto and about the situation of the returning Jews, they advised me to raise with Minsk the question of my working as a representative of the Anti-Fascist Committee in Byelorussia.

I asked them to give me some sort of written note about that. With hints and unfinished sentences they declined to do so. "You know how to say what needs to be said," Itsik Feffer advised me. At the same time, he assured me that my documents would go to the "very top." (Later our material about the returning Jews was actually printed in an internal bulletin of the Central Committee in Moscow.)

At the office of the Byelorussian Central Committee they told me categorically that no representative of the Jewish Anti-Fascist Committee would be permitted in Byelorussia. The leaders of the Anti-Fascist Committee then assigned me to the newspaper *Eynikayt* as special correspondent in Byelorussia. This helped me to observe Jewish affairs up close and to better assess the posibilities that existed in the Soviet Union of healing the deep wounds left by Hitler's murderous crusade against the Jewish people.

Following a meeting at the end of 1945, during which the head of the Soviet Information Bureau, Deputy Foreign Minister Lozovsky, heard a report from the Jewish Anti-Fascist Committee, I came to believe that a catastrophe was approaching for the Soviet Jewish community. (As a representative of *Eynikayt* I had received permission to attend the meeting.) It was during this meeting, in the presence of high military officers and (of course) agents of the Security organs, there was a heated exchange between Itsik Feffer and Peretz Markish, with the most terrible accusations and counter-accusations.

For me it became very clear: A menacing fist was already in position to strike a death blow to the Jewish Anti-Fascist Committee.

It did not happen, however, until almost three years later. When I heard the news about that death blow, I was already in Poland.

The Same Ending . . . But Different

After the uprising in the Warsaw Ghetto and the total destruction of the largest Jewish community in Europe, Hitler proceeded to liquidate all the remaining ghettos. The ghetto in Minsk was one of the last.

How is one to explain why the ghetto in Minsk existed six months longer than the ghetto in Warsaw, longer than the ghettos in Bialystok and Vilna, not to mention many of the smaller ghettos? The question arises especially since the Nazi intentions toward the Soviet Jews were revealed in all their naked brutality in Kiev, the capital of the Ukraine, where the slaughter at Babi Yar took place *immediately after* they occupied the city. The same pattern was followed throughout all the Soviet territories in the Crimea and in the northern Caucasus, in Smolensk and in Byelorussia itself, where the largest Jewish communities were wiped out one after the other.

To some degree, German and Soviet documents give us the answer to the question.

The city of Minsk lay astride the "main highway" of Hitler's military operations during his swift advance toward Moscow; up to the last moment it was a military-administrative center, where a substantial number of German military units were concentrated, particularly those which served — in addition to reserve and defensive functions — as suppliers of materials for the front.

The aforementioned Soviet document concerning the underground resistance movement in Minsk states (page 6) that in Minsk, "there was a permanent military garrison of 5000 troops (including officers); in addition, there were army reserves, the staff of the corps that protected the hinterland of the central front, the S.S. staff and its army, the leaders of the S.D. (*Sicherheitsdienst*), the field police, the Gestapo and intelligence apparatus, and others. Here the Germans had also concentrated their administrative organs — the General-Kommissariat of Byelorussia (headed by Gauleiter Wilhelm Kube), the regional Kommissariat and the Minsk City Kommissariat."

This massive occupation force needed services and labor power. The

Minsk ghetto became the main supplier of forced labor for this multiplicity of military and civilian units, as well as the factories that had not been evacuated or destroyed. The Jews in Minsk, during all the years after the establishment of Soviet power, were predominantly manual laborers, many of them highly skilled — and not only in the "traditional" Jewish crafts.

This situation was noted in a previously cited German document. The highest government authority in Berlin took this into account when it issued its directive that the Jewish craftsmen were to be temporarily spared. At the same time, the Nazi authorities in Minsk, by various means, isolated the Jewish craftsmen from the rest of the ghetto population, especially after Jewish workers suddenly began "disappearing." (The underground ghetto organization was systematically leading groups out into the partisan forests.) In addition to the order creating a separate "specialists zone" in the ghetto — a decree that was in large measure sabotaged by the ghetto underground — the isolation was attempted by "Kasernirung," that is, by keeping the Jewish craftsmen at their work-places overnight. When some Jews learned to overcome this roadblock too, the Nazis kept Jewish workers under armed guard, using the notorious methods perfected in the concentration camps.

The German Jews in the "Hamburg" ghetto were in a somewhat more privileged situation at the beginning, due to the "liberal" attitude of General-Kommissar Kube toward them. Because of this a sharp conflict developed between Kube and the S.S., who complained to Berlin. In all the civil institutions, including his own office, Kube employed mainly German Jews and even created a special enterprise for them. This situation lasted until the July 1942 massacres, when the "Hamburg" ghetto was liquidated. (This ghetto played no role in providing the Germans with craftsmen, since the Jews there were mostly middle-class and intellectuals.)

Along with the general effort of the Nazis to safeguard the Jewish craftsmen for their own labor needs goes the fact — unique to the Minsk ghetto — that the German liquidation "actions" went on continuously, without interruption, from the very beginning. In all the other large ghettos there were periods of "quiet" that lasted for months. The Minsk ghetto was continuously subjected to destructive raids and localized pogroms on certain streets. These day and night attacks systematically wiped out large sections of the ghetto population. The unremitting fear of these sudden attacks, by day and by night, created an extremely tense atmosphere that was unique to the Minsk ghetto. In this situation, the inventiveness of the ghetto Jews in constructing hiding-places reached a high level of technical perfection.

A number of essential factors relating to the Jewish population of Minsk,

[165]

its pre-war history and the conditions of the German occupation determined specific characteristics of the ghetto in that city.

First of all, the Soviet Jews — in contrast to the Jews in Poland and Western Europe — had been deliberately cut off from sources of information that would have made them aware of the mortal threat represented by Hitler fascism. The Jews of Minsk did not know, for example, about the "Night of Broken Glass" (*Kristallnacht*) in Germany; they did not know about the mass expulsion of Polish Jews to Zbonszyn; they did not know about the plan of annihilation in Hitler's *Mein Kampf*, or of the Wannsee decisions regarding the "Final Solution." Two weeks prior to Hitler's invasion of the Soviet Union the Soviet government officially denied the existence of just such a danger. This denial disoriented the Soviet population in general and had a lulling effect on the Jews.

The silence of the entire Soviet propaganda apparatus regarding the Hitler terror inside Germany itself and in the occupied countries of Western and Eastern Europe, dulled the vigilance of the Jews, a substantial number of whom — especially of the older generation — believed that "these were the same Germans" who occupied Minsk during the First World War and that a way would be found to "get along with them." During the first ghetto days I even heard people say that the terror in Minsk was temporary, that it was due to the unrestricted power of the German military.

Psycho-political disorientation was a distinctive characteristic of the Jews in the Minsk ghetto.

Second, the absolute disorientation and helplessness of the Minsk Jews in organizing forms of *internal* ghetto life under the unceasing German terror stemmed from the Soviet past, from the liquidation of any expression of Jewish communal or cultural life in the 1930s.

In all the ghettos in Eastern Europe the model of the Jewish Council (*Judenrat*) was the pre-war Kehillah, which was organized on the basis of political parties. In Minsk, not only was there no remnant of a Kehillah, but no Soviet-Jewish organizations existed whose leaders could have served as a core in establishing the Judenrat. In any case, the Minsk ghetto was the only one where the Judenrat was selected directly by the occupying power, and even this was done completely at random.

It so happened that the people selected by the Germans to serve as a Judenrat were honest, decent men who were really concerned about the ghetto Jews and — up to March 1942 — were an organized part of the resistance organization of the ghetto. The manner of organizing the Judenrat in Minsk, its departments and labor institutions, was in accordance with Soviet organizational patterns and Soviet nomenclature.

[166]

There were no political parties in the Minsk ghetto. Although the underground combat organization at first began its organization according to Communist Party patterns, primarily by recommending people who were politically trustworthy, this pattern very quickly went by the board. The sole criterion for membership in an underground cell, or in a group that was going into the forest, was a recommendation by activists who were themselves trustworthy. Because of the critical role played in this process by the underground activists — who were usually from Poland or Lithuania — there was no antagonism whatsoever between the "easterners" (vostotshnikes) and the "westerners" (zapodnikes) in the Minsk ghetto up to the moment when power over the ghetto was given to the Gestapo "operatives" headed by two refugees from Poland — Epstein and Rosenblatt.

The fact that there were no political parties in the Minsk ghetto hastened the process of consolidating the resistance movement and overcoming the differences between the "western" leaders — who believed that in the ghetto conditions no "okay from above" was needed on the why's and how's of organization — and the "eastern" leaders — who had grown accustomed to acting only on such orders. This attitude, which at first was an obstacle toward the creation of an all-Minsk resistance center, was changed with the help of the ghetto underground leaders.

There were no "class distinctions" in the Minsk ghetto, as there were in other ghettos. There was no obvious separation into rich and poor. Soviet social and economic policy had tended to "equalize" the social status of the population in general, including the Jews. This factor led, however, to a situation where death from hunger and disease rose sharply in the second year of the occupation, that is, as soon as the people in the ghetto ran out of reserves to barter for food. What became decisive for the Jews of Minsk was where you worked for the Germans and the quantity of food you could get there. Combined with the terror, this explains why there were no businesses, cafes, cabarets, theaters, as there were in other ghettos. It was simply impossible.

There was no sign of a cultural life in the Minsk ghetto. First, because of the discriminatory practices of the Soviet government, the Jews were no longer accustomed to having their own cultural life; there was no initiative to organize any such activities in the ghetto even if it had been possible. Second, in an atmosphere of perpetual fear of one's life it was impossible to think about such things. In the early months of the ghetto, religious Jews attempted to form a small congregation, particularly for the High Holidays, but this too had to be abandoned because of the danger of sudden attacks by the Nazis.

[167]

During the summer, behind locked gates, people would gather in the courtyards of their buildings in the evening to exchange "a Yiddish word." Here you could tell who had once studied in a *heder* or who had graduated from a Yiddish elementary school or the Minsk Pedagogic Institute, or who was well read in Yiddish literature. On more "peaceful" evenings, seated on the cobblestones, people nostalgically recited the poems of Izzy Charik, Axelrod and other Yiddish poets.

Beginning in mid-August 1941 there was an underground organization in the Minsk ghetto which gradually worked out a structure, defined its goals and methods of struggle, and tried to make them reality. Although this structure was virtually conspiratorial — cells of five to ten people — the message of the leadership from the very start was that one must remain hidden from the enemy or from suspicious-looking persons, but not from the ordinary Jew in the ghetto. To him one must explain things, and from him one must learn what is most important and most urgent in the conditions under which we were living.

It was not easy to train the basic cadres of the ghetto underground in the principles of conspiratorial work, which were almost second nature to the activists from the West — Haim Alesandrovitsh, Meir Feldman, Cesia Madeisker, Abraham Shliachtovitsh, Reuben Haibloom, Henek Zucker and myself. To the Soviet Jew of the younger and middle generations these principles were completely foreign. This was the principal reason for many of the failures, especially when the "Operative Group" began shadowing our people.

The connection of the underground with the first Judenrat, with its officials in various work-places and with significant sectors of the ghetto population, gradually created a situation where legends began circulating about the "secret leadership" of the organization. In line with concepts that were engrained in the Soviet mentality, our leadership came to be seen as having been "assigned" by Moscow, no more and no less . . . One positive result of this fiction was that people took our warnings and our appeals to heart. This confidence, in turn, helped us in formulating the slogans and objectives for which we had to fight.

It was not easy, though, to convince Jews of the correctness of our main slogan: "Ghetto means death! Break down the fences of the ghetto!" This conviction began to take hold among certain sections of the Jews only after the massacres that took place early in 1941, when the illusion about the Germans of the First World War began to burst. After the entire Niemiga neighborhood was cut off from the ghetto and people began to realize that we had warned about this ahead of time, people began asking us: "What shall we do? How can we break down the fences of the ghetto?"

Finding at least a partial answer to this question became the essence of the resistance movement in the Minsk ghetto until the last day of its existence. In the work of saving women, children and old people, and in leading combat-ready groups into the partisan ranks we saw the main content of Jewish resistance to the Nazis.

From this position came our many-sided efforts to achieve practical results: finding homes for Jewish children on the "Russian side," getting the children there, mass production of documents, work passes, personal papers for the women, and also for young men who, in accordance with Soviet practice, were not circumcized. And also, by looking for forest bases where old people, women and children could be settled. The result of all this was the formation of the Jewish partisan detachment headed by Sholem Zorin.

Unlike the experience in other ghettos, there were no discussions at all in the Minsk ghetto about whether to stay in the ghetto with the rest of the Jews, that is, to look upon the ghetto as the *only* Jewish fighting base, or to join the partisans in the forest. In keeping with the historical experience of the Minsk Jews during the civil war years of 1918-19, when separate Labor Zionist, Bundist and Jewish Communist units were organized to resist the pogromchiks, and when Jews fought in the ranks of the partisan detachments of the time, the partisan struggle against Hitler's killers was regarded as a natural way of participating in the anti-fascist war, of attacking the enemy in his own very sensitive hinterland. The large number of Jews with military training and experience — both men and women — as well as the proximity of the great forests, was another important factor in this decision.

The efforts of the ghetto underground to unite as many combat-ready Jews as possible in the partisan ranks were fulfilled by sending groups from the ghetto into general partisan detachments (first to the east of Minsk) and then to special bases that had been organized by the ghetto underground itself. These Jewish groups developed into effective fighting units. The Jews of the Minsk ghetto were among the first organizers of the great partisan movement in Byelorussia.

The view that going into the forest was a way of saving one's own skin was definitely unjustified. As our census showed, half of the Minsk Jewish partisans died in direct armed struggle against the Germans. However, this was the heroic death of soldiers, of avengers, a death for which everyone who joined the armed struggle was ready.

In the ghetto underground we considered the diversionary and intelligence-gathering work inside Minsk itself as a basic aspect of Jewish resistance. In many German work-places — most of which were of a military nature — the members of our organization (who were often sent in specifically by our people in the Labor Exchange) carried out both slow, "unspectacular" sabotage and major diversionary acts that killed hundreds of German officers and soldiers. One such diversionary act was organized in the brewery, where poison was put into the alcohol production that had been marked for shipment to the German "middle front."

The intelligence reports that we received from important military sites, the maps and plans that were smuggled out by our people and which we turned over to Slavek-Pobiedit, head of the Minsk center, the information on movements and concentrations of enemy forces, including the Gestapo — all these things played a significant part in the central resistance organization and were sent to the appropriate people in the front lines. One example of this was the intelligence work done by the heroic Jewish sculptor Braser, who penetrated the Gestapo officers' quarters and brought out vital information before he was finally discovered and executed.

The role of the ghetto underground in organizing illegal printing shops and providing partisan units with printing materials was noted by Soviet historians. The first such printing shop, located in a cellar just outside the ghetto, was run by our activist Tshiptshin. Jews doing forced labor in the large Minsk printing plant kept the underground press supplied with paper, ink and other necessities.

The close contacts of the Minsk ghetto with the Russian side, often through family members, was another important factor in the resistance. There were cases where mixed couples from the ghetto went to great lengths to settle in the Russian zone so they could bring other people over. For most of its existence the ghetto combat organization was in close touch with the Minsk center and helped them considerably in expanding its influence in the anti-Nazi struggle on the Russian side.

Of great significance was the medical assistance organized by the ghetto underground for the growing partisan movement. By their self-sacrificing service to the ghetto population, by their disciplined behavior in not divulging to the Germans the existence of contagious diseases, and by their active service in many partisan detachments, the Jewish physicians in the Minsk ghetto wrote a particularly bright chapter in the history of Jewish resistance.

The members of the underground inside the Jewish police (the *Ordnungswach*), headed by Commander Zyama Serebrianski, the people whom we sent into the police — such as Zyama Okun, who was a leader in the Jewish combat organization, such as Aaron Fiterson, who had fought as a partisan in the civil war — these men and others restrained and unmasked those individuals who were "carried away with their role" and began to oppress their own people. After these individuals were warned by the combat organization, the Jews sensed a decided difference in their attitude. Exposing the "Operative Group" also served as a warning to these traitors, who were despised by the entire ghetto population.

Up to the last minute, the "unofficial" Jewish partisan leadership in the forest, headed by former organizers and activists of the combat organization in the Minsk ghetto, worked to establish special bases and to bring people from the ghetto to the forest, to encourage Jews to take part in combat and to collect material help for the partisans on a mass scale.

This Jewish forest leadership, which was joined after liberation by former leaders of the ghetto underground who had come back from the eastern zones, endeavored to help the returning Jewish partisans, as well as people returning from the Russian zone, and to organize some sort of communal and cultural activity in Minsk. These efforts to rebuild Jewish life were met by official opposition and threats and finally by repression.

Years later a mass migration movement to Israel arose in Minsk. Among the Jews of Minsk who came to Israel we joyfully greeted many who had fought against fascism in the ghetto and the forest. Together with all of them we honor and preserve the memory of the murdered Jews, of the members of the ghetto underground and of the forest partisans who fell in the battle.

Years Later — For the Last Time

During all the post-war years I made efforts to go to Minsk. I wanted to visit the graves of friends I had known in the ghetto, to see once more places that were associated with our underground work, to find out how the survivors were faring, and together to recall those who had perished.

Between Warsaw and Minsk, however, there is a border. To cross that border you need a Soviet visa. Close friends in Minsk and Moscow warned me: Better stay in Warsaw. . .

After the murder of Shlomo Mikhoels in Minsk, after the arrest of the Yiddish writers and the pogrom on the surviving Jewish institutions (the Anti-Fascist Committee, Emes Publishers, the newspaper *Eynikayt*) it became unthinkable to go to Minsk. In 1956 I visited the Yiddish poet Jacob Sternberg in Bucharest shortly after he was released from imprisonment. He told me that during his interrogation, the KGB had asked him: "When did you meet with Smolar and what did you arrange to do. . . ?"

In 1961, after the appearance of the Yiddish magazine *Sovetish Heymland*, I received a hint from my friends in Moscow that it was now okay for me to come. I went as an official representative of the Executive Committee of the Society for Polish-Soviet Friendship. My first stop was Minsk.

This was no longer the city I had visited for the first time in the 1920s. There were new thoroughfares, with buildings in the style of socialist realism, whose main concern is the decorated facade. Only the partially destroyed neighborhood of the ghetto remained, wrapped in the gloom of the surviving little houses.

Great was the joy of meeeting my old comrades, who told me that there was now a renewed interest in the history of the underground struggle in Minsk during the German occupation, that in the museum devoted to World War II there was a special exhibit about the ghetto, and that my book was among the items displayed. Participants in the underground struggle were being interviewed. I had a long talk with the historian V. S. Davidova, "fleshing out" her information about that dark time. I also met with Vladimir

Karpov and Ivan Novikov, two Byelorussian writers whose stories include the experience of the ghetto.

In one conversation with friends, we were discussing ways to honor the memory of our fallen comrades and pioneers of the resistance. The name of Slavek-Pobiedit, leader of the Minsk underground center, kept coming up. Who was he, this tall, strong young man that I met in the first days of the ghetto underground? Who was he, this young man whom I had to convince of the absolute importance of creating a centralized body uniting all the separate groups who were working for the same objective — the life-and-death struggle against the Nazi enemy. Who was this man who was always ready to help the fighting ghetto?

We already knew his real name — Issai Kozinietz. We knew that he came from Baku. Historians were busy trying to find biographical details about this man who had first united the resistance groups of railroad workers, government employees, professors, law students, the ghetto organization, the Komorovke region; then later, groups and organizations in all areas of the city.

At first I made no connection between the name Issai and the Jewish names Joshua and Isaiah. Among Russians it was not unusual to find the biblical names Moissaye (Moshe), Yakob (Jacob), Samuil (Shmuel) and others. Yet the puzzle gave me no rest. I hadn't noticed anything about his appearance to indicate that he was anything but Russian. Who knew? Perhaps?

I asked the vibrant Jonah Rodinov, correspondent of the *Folks-shtimme* in Riga, to try to locate Slavek's family and learn everything he could about him. Some time later I received this letter from him:

"I've heard from the sister of Issai Pavlovitch Kozinietz. She writes that only two people are left of her very large family — she and an older brother who lives in Alma Ata on pension. (Her husband is from Mogilev in Byelorussia.) Issai was born Joshua (Yehoshua) in Genichesk, a city on the Sea of Azov, near Crimea, region of Zaporozh in the Ukraine.

"Issai went to school, joined the Komsomol, worked in an oil-field in Batumi, then was sent to a technical school. After Byelorussia was annexed, he was assigned to Bialystok as Chief Engineer of the oil-field there. Issai had a wife and two children, whom he managed to evacuate at the beginning of the war, but both children died on the way. His wife got to Alma Ata, where she later remarried.

"There were three brothers — Misha, Issai and Boris, and two sisters — Rachel and Celia. Anna, their mother, died during the evacuation. Rachel knows a little Yiddish. She says that the writer Ivan Novikov contacted her and she gave him precise information about their Jewish family, but in his stories he doesn't say a single word about it."

[173]

So: The first organizer of the resistance movement against the Nazi occupying power in Minsk, capital of Byelorussia, was a Jew: Issai — Joshua — Kozinietz.

While walking to the cemetery in Minsk, I came to the house at Number 25 Niemiga Street, which had been a central meeting place for the leaders of the Minsk combat organization. It was through the window at Number 25 that I jumped when the Gestapo came pounding on the door at midnight. My friend Nikolai never got to the window. I wanted very much to look at the apartment from the inside, to see the place where I received the directives from the Byelorussian partisan staff and the window through which I jumped.

But I soon lost all desire to do so. . .

In the courtyard in front of the apartment a group of schoolchildren on an "excursion" had just arrived. Their teacher began explaining to them what this particular apartment represented; she told them about the role of the "landlord," Nikolai, his wife Tanya and their eleven-year-old daughter Lucia. She described the midnight raid of the Gestapo and the arrest of the whole family, who were burned alive by the Nazis. Only one person escaped, she said, a man name Skromni.

Her story was interrupted by a hoarse scream. From the ground-floor room on the left an old woman ran out, her hair dishevelled, her staring eyes spewing hatred. Pointing to Nikolai's apartment she howled:

"Because of a zhid, because of *one* zhid, they were all killed!"

And the "zhid" — that is, me — stood nearby and did not hear one word from the school-teacher — who was telling the children everything that had happened in that apartment — not one word to counteract the Jew-hating poison with which they were greeted by the neighbor of the Gerasimenko family.

At least if it had been an isolated incident. . . But in the same city of Minsk, where generations of Jews helped to form its character, its social and cultural views, its way of life; in the same city of Minsk, which witnessed the rise and development of Jewish social and political forces that held high the ideals of social freedom and national equality; in the same city of Minsk, where Jewish sons and daughters gave their lives in the Tsarist prisons and penal colonies and on the barricades of the freedom-struggle; in the same city of Minsk, where Jewish self-defense groups took up arms against the pogroms; in the same city on whose railroad station someone had carved the Yiddish letters MINSK; the city where, on Freedom Square stood the base for a statue of the Jewish worker-hero, Hirsh Leckert; the same city of Minsk whose ghetto underground was one of the first to resist the Nazi enemy in active struggle for vengeance; in that same city of Minsk, with the blessing of the Communist Party and the government, there appeared that shameful, anti-human, anti-Semitic "poem" of the Byelorussian poet Maxim Lushanin, under the innocent title, "Dew on the Wheels," which contains these Goebbels-Streicher lines:

"And we had thought
They all would perish in the mills-of-war,
But they managed to become entrenched
Inside the commissary stores.
They occupied Tashkent.
What a pity all of them
Didn't perish in the war. . . "

This pogrom incitement was reprinted in the main organ of the Central Committee of the Byelorussian Communist Party, *Zviazda*, and in the organ of the Byelorussian Writers Union. The creator of that "call to a pogrom" was immediately rewarded by the government of Byelorussia. Today he is a deputy of the Supreme Soviet of the Byelorussian Republic and Chairman of its Legislative Committee.

With justification, the Jews of Minsk concluded that from such a "legislator" they could expect only laws that deprive Jews of their most elementary civil rights. With justification, these proud, courageous Jews chose the path of dignified national protest: they left a soil that had been poisoned by Jew-hatred and turned their eyes toward the Jewish state.

I left Minsk without even saying goodbye.

With love and nostalgia I think about the Jews there with whom I shared the road of prolonged suffering and desperate struggle.